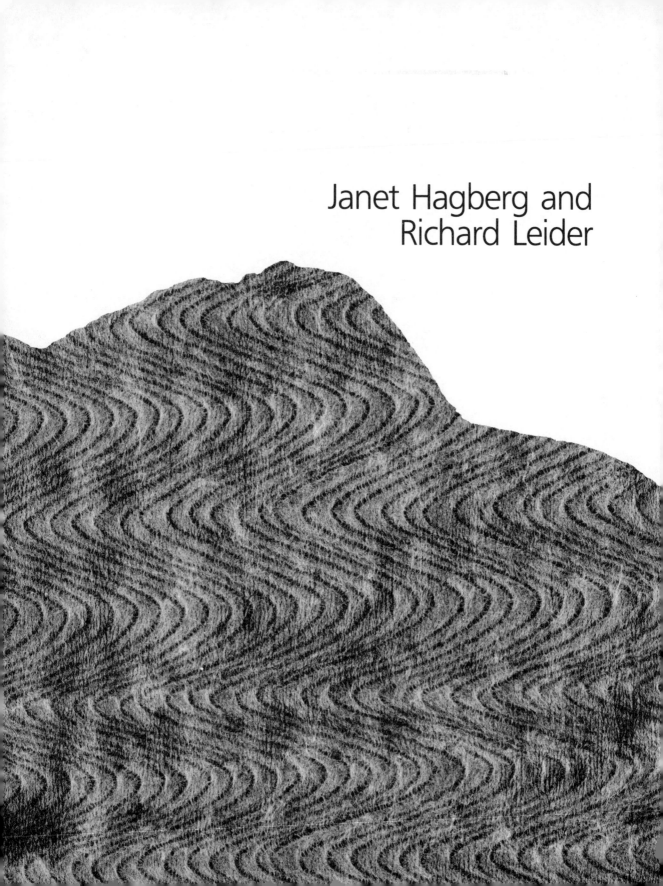

Janet Hagberg and
Richard Leider

The Inventurers

Excursions in Life and Career Renewal

Addison-Wesley Publishing Company
Reading, Massachusetts • Menlo Park, California • New York
Don Mills, Ontario • Wokingham, England • Amsterdam
Bonn • Sydney • Singapore • Tokyo • Madrid • San Juan
Paris • Seoul • Milan • Mexico City • Taipei

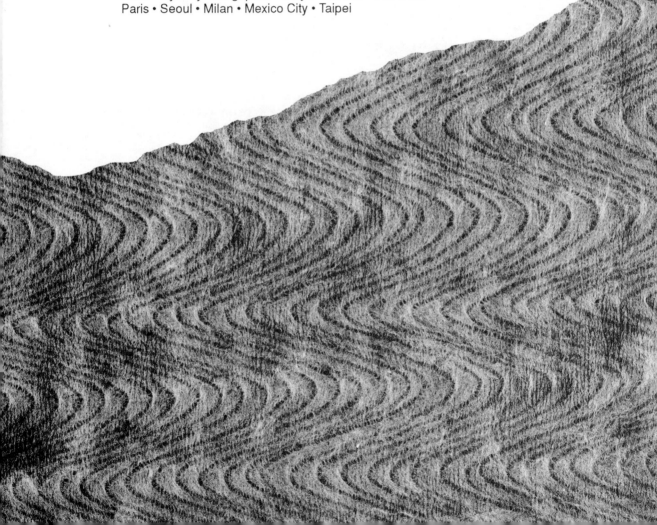

Library of Congress Cataloging in Publication Data

Hagberg, Janet.
    The inventurers : excursions in life and career renewal / Janet Hagberg, Richard Leider.
        p. cm.
    "Third edition"—Pref.
    Bibilography: p.
    ISBN 0-201-09503-3
    1. Self-realization. 2. Conduct of life.   3. Personality and
occupation.   4. Occupations—Psychological aspects.   5. Adulthood.
I. Leider, Richard.   II. Title.
    BF637.S4H33 1988
    158'.1—dc19   88-15477

Portions of this book are adapted with permission from a 3M Company copyrighted program developed by Human Renewal, Inc.

Cover design by Mike Fender
Text design by Joyce Weston
Set in 11 point Frutiger by DEKR Corp., Woburn, Mass.

9101112-CRW-0099989796
Ninth printing, January 1997

Contents

Preface

"The longest journey starts with just one step."

—*Tao Te Ching*

The Inventurers is "just one step" to help you explore new directions, new options in your life and career. We have all thought about taking a step to explore our lifestyle or career dreams. For some of you, life already is a constant discovery of new options. Some of you probably think of your own business enterprise as an avenue to happiness. Others of you, perhaps satisfied with your careers, will explore new leisure pursuits as an opportunity for fulfillment. Still others of you dream of an escape from it all—from the constraints, politics, or career impasses. Yet despite dreams, wishful thinking, and even plans, few people actually take "just one step" toward exploring their dreams. Why is this? Is there a special type of person who is inclined to step forward? Do special characteristics or conditions stimulate the process of life and career renewal? The answers to these questions are the heart of this book.

There is an old adage that "there is only one way to eat an elephant—one bite at a time!" Taking that first bite, or the first step, is what *The Inventurers* is all about. This book shares a life and career renewal process designed to help you find out, step by step, what you want out of your life and career, then expand and explore your options. The key word is "process." You will learn a process that you can use now, in six weeks, or in two years for developing your own practical system of life and career renewal. The process in this book has grown out of life and career renewal experiences with a wide range of adult groups in business and industry, education, and government.

The words "life" and "career renewal" deserve some explanation.

You will see these words often in this book. When those separate words are put together as "life and career renewal," the phrase means *the process* of periodically reassessing your lifestyle and work style in order to reflect and focus on new options that might make you more satisfied.

The word "career" in our society often connotes a demanding, rigorous, preordained life pattern to whose goals everything else is ruthlessly subordinated. In contrast, the word "career" in this book connotes meaningful and stimulating activity (paid or unpaid) whose goals include excitement, challenge, and personal satisfactions.

This book is designed as a practical tool for you to use in your own life and career renewal experiences. It should be a personal book, since each of your experiences will be uniquely yours. The tools help you plan, shape, and map your life and career options. Like any tools, they can be used skillfully or clumsily; they can be unused or misused. The way you use these tools depends on your preferred style. Different people learn in different ways. Before you start the process, you may want to review the ways others have used it:

- Read through the entire book systematically, stopping to do the exercises at the appropriate spots along the way. Complete one section (or chapter) at a time, taking time out to reflect and to write down your insights.
- Scan the book to get an overall understanding of the process. You can get an overview of the entire book in an hour or less. Then go back and do the exercises or read the chapters that seem appropriate.
- Read the book with a friend, spouse, or co-worker. Discuss the exercises, comparing your responses and insights, or tape your responses and share the tapes.
- Read the book as part of a course, project, or structured learning effort. If a structured class is not available, create your own! Set up timetables and systematic ways to share your experiences with the group.

There is a story of a man who set a speed record for hiking the Appalachian Trail. Upon completion, he observed that he would like to do it over again—but this time at his leisure because he hadn't seen anything! A key to this renewal process is complete information and experience gathering, and that often takes time and reflection. There is no great rush to get to the end. Take your time and enjoy every step of this unique process. T. S. Eliot sums it up in "Little Gidding,": "We shall not cease from exploration/And the end of all our exploring/Will be to arrive where we started/And know the place for the first time."*

This book is based on several assumptions about people. The process in the book reflects these assumptions:

1. *Coping with change*. We all have different styles of coping with "present shock"—the accelerating change around us. Some of us ignore it, others try to stop it, some of us run from it, and others try to change along with it. You need to learn what your style is and how to use it effectively.

2. *Untapped abilities*. Psychologist William James said that "95 percent of us live on 5 percent of our potential." You possess much untapped potential that could change your life considerably.

3. *Self-direction*. The basic ingredient in life and career renewal is *choice*—the choice of taking responsibility for yourself. In any situation, you have basically two options: change the situation or change the mindset that is perceiving the situation. The choice is yours alone. Many of us are more comfortable allowing others to make the choices, until we really experience the way that self-direction mobilizes us with enthusiasm and ingenuity.

4. *Organized planning*. Effectively assessing life and career renewal options requires more than new insights and awareness of your life. Your reflections must be organized and focused into an action plan in order to contribute to satisfying progress. And self-discipline is a virtue. We may have a wealth of planning skills, but seldom use them for our personal lives. If you put your planning skills to work with a process that is practical, you will be sure to make progress.

5. *Risk taking*. Choices involve risks. Risk is the element in career or life

---

* T.S. Eliot, *Collected Poems 1909–1962* (New York: Harcourt Brace Jovanovich, 1970).

that everyone wishes would go away. The idea that a life or career can be planned, predictable, and risk-free is, of course, not reality. The inventuring process emphasizes a balance between the need to plan and realize goals and the need to spontaneously live life as it unfolds.

And now we offer you that first step!

J. H.
R. L.

Minneapolis, Minnesota
March 1978

Preface to the Third Edition

Three themes that emerge most strongly for us in this edition are balance, harmony, and purpose, both in our lives and in our careers. These are most certainly themes in our own lives but also major themes in the lives of people we hear from in all work settings. At almost any age, be it twenty-five, forty-five, or sixty-five, these three ideas emerge as central issues. Behind these themes we believe is a spiritual quest for wholeness and a longing for peace of mind.

The level of anxiety in our world today is high. The morale is low. We are in a transition time and our future direction is evolving. We offer this edition as a path of reflection amidst the anxiety, as a way to become more aware of who we are and what our purpose is.

We offer you a few reflection statements as we continue the excursion together. They are, in our opinion, "excruciatingly simple":

- The quality and depth of our relationship to ourselves is the mirror that all other relationships reflect; we must be in touch with our feelings because they tell us who we really are.
- We need solid support systems that can carry us through the various passages of life.
- We must first make necessary "life" decisions, which are the raw material of "career" decisions.
- In the final analysis, living with integrity is the bottom line; integrity comes mainly from simple, daily acts—acting consistently on our deepest values.

J. H.
R. L.

Minneapolis, Minnesota
January, 1988

Acknowledgments

The inventuring model has been a fascinating one to see unfold. From the beginning it seemed to have an energy and an urgency of its own. Bits and pieces have continued to emerge in the decade or so of our advising and consulting with organizations and individuals dealing with career renewal and change.

We are grateful to the people whose lives we have observed over the years in order to write this book, the hundreds of people whose real experiences are reflected in these pages. We are also thankful for colleagues in the career development field and other fields who have inspired us, challenged us, and supported us. We would especially like to acknowledge Richard Bolles, whose *What Color Is Your Parachute?* led the way for us all, and Betty Olson, our colleague, who has supported our work for over twelve years, and has let us use ideas from her fine work in career development: the spiritual life line and job criteria worksheet.

The Life Inventure

1   The Inventurers

Many of us go through life not clear about what we want, but pretty sure that this isn't it! This book presents a process, first to assist us in finding out what we want and then to explore lifestyle and career directions. It is difficult to take charge and create our own challenges to get ourselves moving again when we are frustrated and dulled by our current situations. But we must! Learning to create our own new challenges and options rather than waiting for them to happen to us is a special value of this process. We discover new inner resources and capacities we might never have realized we had in our ordinary situations simply because the capacities were never called on. We discover new interests, directions, and careers. As Abraham Lincoln said, "People are just about as happy as they expect to be." It is up to us. Life is a daily proposition.

The expectations with which we start each morning determine the results we achieve. Life can produce fulfillment and happiness. Every day offers the "inventurer" an opportunity to see some aspect of life in a novel way. What's an "inventurer"? What does "inventuring" mean? *Webster's Dictionary* does not list these words. You will find "adventuring"—"to venture or to take a risk; as adventuring upon paths unknown." Well, "inventurer" and "inventuring" are new words.

AN INVENTURER

You are an inventurer if you are one of that special breed of people who takes charge and creates your own challenges to get yourself moving. More specifically, you are an inventurer if you are willing to take a long look at yourself and consider new options, venture inward, and explore. You are an inventurer if you see life as a series of changes, changes as growth experiences, and growth as positive. You are inventuring on life's *excursions* and learning about yourself as a result. You may feel lonely at times, and get discouraged for a while. But you are willing to risk some disappointments and take some knocks in your quest because you are committed to a balanced lifestyle and to more than just making a living. You are part of a group of people who want to make a living work. If you have these qualities, you are an inventurer.

Inventurers are people who choose to take a fresh look in the mirror to renew and perhaps recycle their lifestyles and careers. Some inventurers, seemingly snug in life and career patterns, are exploring their "greener pastures" or "South Sea island" dreams in search of their own personal Declaration of Independence: the pursuit of happiness. Other inventurers are planning second careers or early retirements. Some are underemployed and seeking careers more integrated with their abilities and lifestyles. They are female and male and old, young, and in between. Let's meet several of them:

CASE STUDY

Peter is a forty-three-year-old manager in the data-processing department of a large corporation. He hit a plateau, a flat place in his career, and described it like this: "I hated my job, but I couldn't let go. I was scared just thinking about the options. I had seventeen years invested in the company. I was married and responsible for three teenagers. I had a nice home and plenty of expenses. I was trapped—boxed in. I felt like a 'meal ticket.' And besides, I didn't know what my bargaining power was at forty-three—after all I wasn't as sharp as those young MBA's."

Peter was not a depressed failure. His comments highlight a number of personal conflicts shared by responsible people in the corporate world. Overlapping personal, family, and business pressures force us to reassess our priorities because they challenge personal value systems. And the current climate in which Peter and other professionals must resolve their dilemmas is full of ambiguity and contradiction.

Peter's success, so apparent to others, felt unfulfilling to him. Success *without* fulfillment is a common midlife phenomenon. Although he had achieved external success, inside he felt fearful and anxious and had lost his sense of confidence.

He asked himself: "What has happened to me?" "What am I doing with my life and work?" "How did I get stuck like this?"

Peter is part of all of us, and that's frightening. But only a small part. As ambiguous as things appeared to him, he still had options and he knew it. He remained optimistic about his future. By instinct and insight he recognized the balance between security and risk. He held on to known advantages that limited his fulfillment, instead of taking risks that might rekindle the aliveness he sought.

Like everyone else, Peter was not immune to the personal, economic, and relationship pains we all experience. As he stated, "I wasn't looking for a panacea. I was just trying to find a reasonable balance. I was working my tail off—for what?"

And now . . . Peter's wife, Judith, has returned to college. In making that decision, she has become much more enthusiastic about life and is usually gone a couple of evenings a week, to the library or to participate in a seminar. Her shift in focus has caused Peter to take some positive steps as well.

Though physically trim and fit-looking, Peter had complained of chronic tiredness for several months. On the advice of his physician, after having a complete physical, Peter changed his diet and exercise program. He has now joined a tennis league, walks a mile most evenings after work, and has cut drinking out almost entirely. He prides himself on wearing the same size suit now as he did when he got out of the Army.

Disagreement about money was a recurrent theme in Peter and Judith's marriage. A visit to a financial planner helped them agree on some mutual goals and pare down their expenses. As a result, they have also started thinking about a "Plan B"—an early-retirement option in a mountain area they both love. They've planned their next vacation to spend a month visiting and researching that area.

Perhaps the greatest void for Peter was his lack of close friends. He had an abundance of acquaintances but a poverty of friendships. This bothered him to the point that he decided to schedule one lunch a week with a friend, just for friendship and to check in with each other!

Peter's energy seems to be returning, even though his career path and job have stayed the same. He still has a nagging sense of malaise, but he feels that he's spending his time well exploring other parts of his life.

CASE STUDY

Pat is a thirty-two-year-old marketing research professional in a medium-size company. She's been with this company five years. She is an MBA and is hard-driving and determined to succeed. Her job requires her to travel a great deal. From the beginning, Pat and her husband, Steve, an attorney, were forced to deal with balancing self, marriage, and work.

"I know my family life is important, but at this point I have to put my major effort into my job, otherwise I won't succeed. These are the crucial years that will guarantee us a good life later on." Pat feels that time is on her side, that there will be plenty of time and that someday they can make up for what they missed earlier.

Steve says, "I'm concerned about both of our careers, but I also want us to grow together! We may have to postpone some job opportunities in order to lead a more meaningful life. I know we can't have it all."

Trying to strike some practical balance between them is the real pressure. What are they to do? Pat has needs, the organization has needs, and Steve has needs. And they don't have the same goals and timetables in mind at any one time.

The answers aren't clear-cut. Someone will likely get the short end of the stick, maybe Pat.

In addition, Pat faces social pressures. No one asks Steve how it feels to be a successful partner in a law practice and at the same time how it feels to deal with the problems of being a husband. But everyone poses that kind of question to Pat. Besides, the community supports Steve's role, but subtly questions hers. "Pat is away on a business trip" is often met with raised eyebrows.

Pat's father was a lawyer, and her mother, a public school teacher. Both urged her to prepare a career for herself and they stressed the importance of economic independence. She's working hard at her marriage and the interdependence required for a shared life.

We are educated for our careers but not for our marriage and family life. Pat is aiming to go to the top. But she already feels overloaded and begins to wonder what the personal cost will be if she goes for it. Pat and Steve are doing a personal audit, asking themselves not only "Who am I?" but "Who are we?" "What do we want?" "Is what I want realistic?" "What is the cost to me? To us?"

Pat's most frequent complaint is that events seem so much beyond her control. "Yeah, I'm successful. All my college friends wish they had my freedom, my opportunities. I surely don't want their world, but I'm not certain I want this one either. I don't know why. Things aren't what I thought they would be."

She complains of restlessness and fatigue and a lack of direction. Recently she began to talk of just traveling for a year or taking a sabbatical.

Pat and Steve attended the church of a friend where they heard a dynamic sermon, "Life's Meaning and Purpose." They made an appointment to talk with the minister, who suggested they attend a weekend marriage enrichment retreat that the church sponsors.

That experience was a breakthrough. Together, for the first time in their married life, they established some mutual goals and a plan to achieve them. They also decided to plan weekly "dates" together on their calendars—often to try new cultural or educational experiences.

They also decided to take quarterly "getaways" to plan and review their mutual game plans. They are taking the first steps to becoming inventurers.

CASE STUDY

Jerry is a fifty-one-year-old laborer caught in the midst of his industry's massive layoffs because of downsizing. He is an autoworker whose family income, with his union wage, overtime, and his wife's work as a secretary, exceeds $45,000 in a good year. He's hung on—a "survivor"—but who knows for how long? "Thinking about losing my job is like thinking about my own death. I know it's going to happen, but I have this angle that maybe I'll escape. Somehow it won't happen to me. Maybe I'll beat it!"

"If I stop too long to think about what's happening at work—layoffs, friends leaving—I get depressed. I'm so tired of the constant changes. I just want to live for now and let the organization worry about the future."

His wife often complains, "Jerry, what's wrong with you? You seem so preoccupied. You're a stranger around here—you're not even here when you're here! What's bugging you?"

Jerry is petrified about his future. It doesn't matter what you call it—downsizing, fired, axed—it feels the same. An uncertain future is the result. He's watched the dismantling of his organization and his long-time work friendships. He's wondering whether he has a real job or whether he'll be next.

In order to survive today in the long or short run, people must be more aware of the organization politics around them. This means knowing who you are and what you are willing to live with.

Jerry says, "I'm not sleeping or eating well these days. I am frightened and depressed and scared. But who do I blame? The company's got to make changes. I have performed well for the company. But I have responsibilities—a wife, and children just about to enter college. I feel like I'm out of control and I don't understand it because I do still have a job. I guess I should feel grateful. But somehow I can't escape the feeling now that it's just not worth it!"

Jerry shares with many other people feelings of being out of control, cut off, impotent; of having become obsolete, of being angry because someone else exercises control over his life. And there is the underlying feeling that if he had been as good as he thought he was, this could have been avoided. He could have escaped it.

He is facing the great taboo: failure. The hard fact is that he may have to settle for less—a reality that no one accepts gladly.

Jerry's reassessing his ambitions. How much risk is he willing to take at this point? Should he hang on or move on? Should he consider making a major career change?

He's taking a career transition course being offered by his union. He thought it was going to be a bore. But during the first session, he realized that he was totally uncertain about his life goals. Here he was, fifty-one years old, still floating along! At first he was depressed, then confused, and then angry. He's beginning to conclude that his work is not what he thought it would be, and he doesn't plan to stay more than another year or so. A key insight Jerry got from the class was understanding that he did have "marketable skills" and that he was not trapped in his industry. He's put together a résumé emphasizing what he can do and is spending Fridays doing information interviewing with small and medium-size businesses. He's interested in transferring his skills into the printing industry and is focusing on that. "I work hard and I have to keep moving, but I'm excited and look forward to new places and new challenges. I just don't think anyone can say what the future will be!"

These inventurers prove what the wise teachers have said for ages: "The knowledge is right in us—all we have to do is clear our minds and open ourselves to see the obvious."

"IF I HAD MY DRUTHERS . . ."

In your search for career/life direction, we'd like to encourage you to dream, to fantasize about the kind of life and career you would like in your future. John Holland, a well-known vocational psychologist, has said that what you most wish to be is the most reliable prediction of your future vocational choice.

Stop for a moment—dream a little! Suppose money were no object and you could do anything or become anyone you chose. What would you do? Where? What is your fantasy?

The hiker or backpacker is an applicable analogy to the inventurer. Inexperienced hikers soon learn the basic, if startling, assumption that they don't know how to walk. It isn't just a matter of putting one foot down in front of the other. There are techniques for hiking—even for resting—that create a more enjoyable experience. Inventurers, too, have techniques that help them cover many miles—and enjoy every one. Those techniques make up the process in this book.

There are several reasons for the ever-increasing popularity of the inventuring experience. First, as it does in the spirit of the hiker on the open road, the romantic spirit of the inventurer lurks in the psyche of every human being. Second, the hiker, on reaching the summit of a distant mountain, and the inventurer, on setting and reaching a goal, have a feeling of happiness and fulfillment. Third, the hiker gets a sense of liberation from escaping the tension and hustle of daily life. The inventurer who discovers more balance in life feels a similar liberation.

Inventuring rekindles the sense of wonder and renewal, the exhilaration of a new challenge. Inventuring, however, is intended to be a pleasure and not an endurance test. Just as experienced hikers, eager to reach their destination, think nothing of hiking fifteen miles a day while toting a thirty-pound pack, an experienced inventurer thinks nothing of embarking on a new learning experience while holding a full-time job, because of the eagerness to discover new interests, directions, and careers.

Hikers plan or map their excursions. They select side trips, check overnight accommodations, tune up their equipment, and start packing. Inventurers extend these same preparations to their own lives. The excursion process in this book contains a special map. It looks exactly like the map in figure 1.1. Turn to your full-size Excursion Map in chapter 18, pages 188–189. This map will serve as a continuing itinerary as you read the book. At the end of exercises and chapters, you will be asked to go to your Excursion Map and log important insights. The arrow

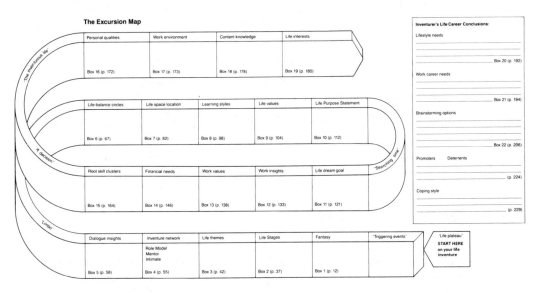

Figure 1.1. *The Excursion Map*

symbol will signal you to turn to your map. When you complete the book, your map will provide a summary of the routes you have created toward new destinations.

 Start now by writing key words from the fantasy you just completed in Box 1 on your Excursion Map on pages 188–189.

Whether or not you use a map depends on your preferred mode of travel, your style. The Excursion Map assists you in charting your own route; it helps you get out of the rut of accepting the usual paths or tried-and-true trails and helps you to begin to discover your own creative routes.

Prepare yourself! We mean to send the blood flowing through your arteries and veins until you are tingling with newly discovered excitement about your options. For inventurers are agents of disturbance. They jog themselves out of their complacency and routines, their ruts. Someone once said, "The only difference between a rut and a grave is the depth of the excavation!" Inventurers prefer neither.

Inventurers—alive, aware, and excited about their lives—are in short supply. For every one who summons up the courage and determination to inventure, there are many more who hesitate, who are afraid, who plod on, waiting for some special moment for a push up the hill! Often these "shelf sitters" simply permit their lives to happen without mapping any direction. Or they make the mistake of trying to live their lives by what somebody else thinks they should be doing, instead of choosing the direction most rewarding to them personally. They seem to subscribe to the old adage, "If you don't know where you're going, any road will probably get you there."

EXCURSION CONTRACT

From time to time throughout this book you will be asked to stop what you are doing, be it reading, thinking, writing, imagining, dreaming, or conjuring, and actually to get a taste of "inventure" by taking a risk and pushing yourself to draw a few conclusions, make a few decisions, and act on them.

Some of you will complain that the excursion process doesn't fit you or your situation or that you can't change, because other people won't let you. If you're going to excuse yourself, at least take personal responsibility and decide you don't *want* to change right now.

Contracting with another person to accomplish something by a certain date is a creative way to stimulate action and overcome the villain—procrastination. At important points throughout the book, there will be contracts for you to complete. The more specific the contract, the better it is and the easier it is to know when it's been completed. It doesn't have to be elaborate, but it must describe what you will do and when you'll do it.

Commitment to clearly stated goals leads to achievement of those goals. Yet achieving commitment is not as easy as it sounds. Obstacles get in your way. Other activities compete for your time. That's why contracts are such helpful tools.

There are some guidelines for making contracts work for you. The most effective contracts are:

1. *Written.* The primary purpose of writing contracts is not so they can be shown to others, but rather to clarify them for you. Once a contract is written, you have more investment in it.
2. *Step by step:* Break your goal down into bite-size pieces.
3. *Time-conscious.* Setting target dates for the completion of each step of a contract provides constant reinforcement and a sense of accomplishment.
4. *Supportive.* Sharing your contract with another person helps you to clarify your thinking, obtain feedback, and generate a commitment to complete the task.
5. *Your own.* Your goals must be your own and be based on your personal values.

Here's your chance to take the first step! Decide with whom you would like to contract—(spouse, friend, co-worker, manager, etc.). Tell them that you are asking for a commitment on their part to help you complete this book. Ask for what you need and the hours it will take the other person to help you stick to this task. Then mark down on your calendar regular times when you will meet. Ask your contract partner to check on your progress and to question you if you've done little or nothing since your previous meeting.

Excursion Contract #1

Dear _____: Date: _____

I am reading a book called *The Inventurers: Excursions in Life and Career Renewal*. The book is really a workbook and a process.

I have decided that an important commitment for me to make is to complete this process. To do that will require support and feedback.

I would like your help in monitoring my progress.

I have decided to complete the process by _____.

(date)

Would you meet with me on _____, _____, and

                                     (date)   (date)

_____ so I can share my progress with you?

(date)

Goal: What I expect to accomplish through the inventure process is:

_____

_____

Getting Going: The steps I need to take to get moving on things are:

1. _____

2. _____

3. _____

4. _____

Thanks for your support.

            Sincerely,

_____

Make a duplicate for your partner

2   The Postponed Life

We live in an age of exploration and adventure. We have reached the moon. Yet it is obvious that the real need for exploration and adventure resides in inner, rather than outer, space.

We are staggered by the rate of accelerating change. Future shock has become "present shock." The rules of the game change constantly. Turn on your television or pick up today's newspaper. "Present shock" leaves some of us immobilized—in a state of suspended animation! With so much change and so many stimuli competing for our attention, we often wonder which way to turn. Often the best we can do is to hold our ground and hang on—as the Fiddler on the Roof proposes, "just trying to maintain our balance."

"Present shock" affects some of us in the opposite way, and we run off in several directions at once, hoping that by trying several approaches to our problems, we might hit on *the* panacea or solution— *the* right mate, *the* right house, *the* right job, *the* right amount of money—to make us happy. Often we become postponers, waiting for *the* solution. As we wait, we do experience some successful moments. But since we haven't mapped out what we're looking for to begin with, each magic solution gradually deteriorates.

In our quest for lifestyle and career solutions, we find that each option satisfies some needs and frustrates others. We are urged to change, but no one has told us how to approach change or how to map our way through the change.

Underlying this phenomenon is a fundamental truth: It is the thought patterns and expectations in our heads that make us unhappy, not the people and conditions outside ourselves (where we usually place the blame!). We have learned to live according to arbitrary expectations set up by the people and conditions in our lives (the infamous "they") rather than to grow according to our own expectations. Further, in our desire to keep up with external expectations, we respond to every new stimulus, trying to keep up with a "they" that doesn't seem to know where "they" are going either. We become so skillful at being *reactive* to "them" that we forget how to be *proactive* in terms of "me."

If you are trying to adapt to external demands rather than discovering your own internal choices, you are setting yourself up as a slave. In fact, if "they" control your expectations and choices, then "they" should be the ones reading this book for you. Inventurers refuse to accept the slave role. They refuse to postpone their lives because of what "they" might think.

Inventurers refuse to live the up-and-down, hour-by-hour "postponed life" that "they" often seduce us to live:

- Wait until I find the right job (mate, house,)—then . . .
- Wait until I get to be a manager (partner, president,)—then . . .
- Wait until I have enough money (salary, savings,)—then . . .
- Wait until the kids are through college, the mortgage paid—then . . .
- Wait until I retire—then . . .

. . . Then I'll start living the way *I* want to, and I'll be happy!

Seconds accumulate into minutes, and the sequence unfolds through hours, days, weeks, months, and years to form the patterns of our lives. As a song by Harry Chapin goes, "there's no ticktock on your electric clock, but still your life runs down." Year by year, the postponed life continues, until we have a whole postponing society looking for new postponement quests as elusive as finding pots of gold at the end of the rainbow.

We fail to grasp that we have 168 hours to live each week—no more, no less. For a thirty-four-year-old with an average life expectancy of seventy-four years, that equals 349,440 hours. Under normal habit patterns, those 349,440 hours look like this:

Sleep	116,480	33%
Work (commuting included)	174,720	50
Maintenance	30,000	11
Free time	28,240	6
	349,440	100%

Just a matter of time! How many hours do *you* expect to live? How do you spend your precious time?

Assuring ourselves that everyone around us also seems to be suffering from "postponement battle fatigue," we lower our expectations and decide that our ideal of happiness is probably not realistic anyway. We lower ourselves into our ruts—the postponed life is deadly!

This raises some curious questions: Why haven't we seriously challenged these patterns? Why is the postponed life so seductive? Why do we expect only small dribbles of happiness? Why do we map out only safe excursions (if we map at all)? It seems that either we're not aware, or we don't know how!

You *do* have options. You *can* choose to take control of your life and design strategies to begin living your life as a player rather than as a spectator. Instead of following someone else's map or fumbling around with no map at all, you can learn the skills to make change work for you creatively, one step at a time. To do this, you need to perceive clearly who you are and exactly what are the *real* conditions of your life. To achieve this clear perception takes steady work on these key questions:

1. Who am I?
2. Who is in control of my life?
3. What kind of lifestyle or balance in my life would make me happiest?
4. What role does spirituality play in my life?
5. What skills and abilities do I have and most enjoy using?
6. Where and to what life purpose do I want to apply my skills?

7. What options (or possibilities) fit my wants?
8. How do I go about locating or creating situations for the options I choose?
9. What holds me back from making changes?

POSTPONEMENT AND WORK DILEMMAS

Often we postpone becoming who we really are and who we want to be because we feel we are caught in circumstances beyond our control in the work setting. Suppose we are in the baby boom generation. We feel we will never get ahead because there are so many more people with whom to compete and contend. Suppose we are white males. We are now frustrated because we have to compete with so many more women and minorities who have the same education and experience we have. Suppose we are victims of a layoff because of a takeover. We blame the current business climate for squashing our jobs. Or let's say we've plateaued in our career, hit a point where we feel less excited, unchallenged, and stuck in the security of our work. We don't have the energy to take a risk to change or leave, and somehow we hope the organization will do something. Perhaps we've worked in the nonprofit world for a long time because we believed in service and now we are starved for a new challenge and burned out on people. Maybe we had a chance for early retirement because of company restructuring and we didn't take it because we didn't know what we would do with our time.

All of these situations are very real to the people involved and all are examples of living a postponed life. Whenever we have a tendency to blame someone else or a situation for our lot in life we are handing over our power to them and giving up our risk-taking ability. There is always a way to move or grow if we are willing to look closely inside ourselves instead of only at the external situation.

The excursion process in this book helps you deal more effectively with these situations. As a process, it is new, but many of the components have been tried and tested for thousands of years. Answering the personal questions and resolving the work dilemmas is part of the process. The questions are ones that all of us must ask and answer for ourselves in our own way. You have probably noted the amazing sources of energy available to people who have dealt with these questions, people who have a purpose. The world stands aside for a person with a plan!

Clearly, inventuring poses risks. But choosing not to inventure in an age of "present shock" may also be risky. Quite a few people who do not want to be pulled in a new direction now may in a few years find themselves pushed in one. Our fear of failure often keeps us from risking. There is usually no learning without some fumbling and failure. It's as simple as that! Life's too short for you not to be an inventurer. Marcus Aurelius (121–180 A.D.) wrote, "[People] seek out retreats for themselves in the country, by the seaside, on the mountains, and thou too art wont to long above all for such things. But nowhere can a [person] find a retreat more full of peace than one's own soul. Make use then of this retirement continually and regenerate thyself."

3   The Inventurous Life

Wake up! Or be awakened hastily by the events around you. It's time to choose your own excursion. Awakening to the "inventurous life," we often realize that we have been asleep—postponing life or perhaps calculating it rather than living it! Asleep, we did not understand what life is all about. Awake, we now see choices that we never knew were open to us before. We were not aware that a real problem in our lives involves how consciously we are using our minds. Asleep, our lives were random patterns of events to be avoided. We did not realize that we were asleep; we did not see how life could be any different. Asleep, we believed that life should live up to our expectations, should be "this way" or "that way." Asleep, we drifted off into postponement: "When I get it all together in the future, then I'll start living, but until then . . ." All of a sudden we wake up to find that as Sam Levinson states, "When I finally got the means to an end, they moved the ends further apart."

Inventurers have discovered the secret—the wake-up call of the inventurous life. Inventurers know the difference between assuming personal responsibility for their every action, thought, feeling, or situation and assuming that they are caught up in actions over which they have no control. Here are some examples.

CASE STUDY

Jack is a fifty-four-year-old college biology professor. His awareness that he had arrived at a kind of plateau began when his son patted the back of his head and said, "Dad, you're getting bald." It was not just aging. After five decades of clearing the academic hurdles, learning to teach, learning what it meant to be married, he realized that an era of his life was over. His feelings were imprecise: "How shall I spend the balance of my life?" Feeling too comfortable with his current challenges, he mentioned his dilemma to his department head. To his astonishment, he received an intensely negative reaction. "Was my willingness to disclose my uncertainties so threatening to him that he could only react by attacking me? How could anybody as fortunate as I am have questions about my life? What is wrong with me?"

Nothing, of course. Jack came to understand that the feelings he thought were unique to him were, in fact, universal. He formed a support group in the university community for other staff people who were struggling with aspects of the fifty-plus dilemma. He published several articles on this topic and gave several speeches to local business groups. His reputation spread. He developed a course on adult development with a colleague from the psychology department. He found that he had uncovered a strong need in his community. He applied for and received a fellowship to study adult-counseling practices. He has now returned to the university and has a half-time teaching appointment. With the other half of his time, he's opened a counseling practice. He's so excited that he can hardly wait to get up every morning!

———————————

Sooner or later it happens to most of us. As Sam Keen, author of *What to Do When You're Bored and Blue*, observes, "We wake up one morning, the tide is out, and nothing is visible except mud flats." The excitement of living has sunk! We go through the day postponing life, more like spectators than players.

The condition is common. James Thurber's word "slish" sounds like the way it feels—somewhere between "slush" and "ish"! The postponed life has become the common cold of the psyche. The combination of too many options, too much advice, and no guidelines turns normal change into a crisis. When we feel overwhelmed with life, we define it as a crisis. We postpone!

Psychologist John Brantner cited the following lines written by an anonymous author as a guide to living:

When we are depressed or discouraged or anxious,
When we are embarrased or ashamed,
When we are taken by surprise
These are the three surest signs
    That we are in a situation
That offers the opportunity for growth.

Life is an upward spiral, a series of excursions, of highs and lows. Anyone can handle the high points. The big moments take care of themselves. It's the valleys and plateaus, the postponements, that we must learn to handle. Nothing could be more normal than these plateaus and valleys; they are inevitable parts of human existence. But what is not normal is the way in which we cope with them.

Most of us realize that a crisis that is dealt with successfully creates growth and increases our sense of self-esteem. But what we do not know is how to meet crises (or perhaps even create them) in a positive way.

We cannot begin to make real changes in our lives—begin to work toward the happiness that is our birthright—until we begin to understand crises as a key to growth. Crises often herald a new stage of growth! Consider:

Writers: Virginia Woolf and Eugene O'Neill
Artists: Paul Gauguin and Georgia O'Keeffe
Architects: Frank Lloyd Wright and Charles Luckman
Visionaries: Mother Theresa and Mahatma Gandhi
Political leaders: Anwar Sadat and Golda Meir

All went through profound crises and then made tremendous creative gains, often accomplishing their best work. These people all grew significantly in the midst of periods of intensive change in their lives. Their "lost" periods of time were often their most productive. It was as if they stumbled into greatness!

THE EXCURSION MODEL: STAGES OF CHANGE

In achieving growth, we experience rather predictable sequences. Change follows this sequence of stages:

Stage I—Life Plateaus

Life seems to be running pretty smoothly for us. Everything seems in good working order. We may be generally satisfied with our lifestyles, relationships, careers. We could identify with Jack, the professor mentioned earlier, for whom things weren't going badly; they were just going. In this stage we might tend to narrow the scope and variety of our lives. Of all the exciting options we might pursue, we settle on a fixed few. We can become set in our ways. Then self-oblivion sets in. We lose the capacity to see what is before us, lose our freshness of perception. We postpone!

Stage II—Triggering Events

Suddenly things change—voluntarily or involuntarily. We are knocked off balance by a turn of events that reveals new problems. The most common triggering events are death, divorce, a job change, a health change, spiritual awakening, a physical move, new relationships, change in habits, deep loss, change in children's lives, retirement, therapy, decade birthdays, (thirty, forty, fifty). Triggering events are those "moments of truth" or revelations we all experience on occasion. These "awakening" events can act as catalysts to our own change and renewal. They are our wake-up calls. They may be startling, or we may just soberly decide one day that we can't continue in the same way.

Stage III—Limbo

To insulate ourselves against the shock of abrupt change, we often go into a sort of suspended animation or limbo. We withdraw emotionally.

Limbo is a feeling of knowing what your life isn't going to be in the future, but not having any notion of what it is going to be, feeling immersed in the "slish." Being in limbo is being immobilized—trapped, without options, not knowing in which direction to turn. In time, limbo becomes boring and frustrating. We feel we must do something—act, do anything to escape from our dilemma!

Stage IV—Searching Time

We explore solutions—counseling, a personal-growth workshop, a new relationship, a book, a job change, travel, friends, ideas, a geographical move. We know the answer is out there somewhere; we just have to find it. It's just around the corner, in the next course, in a new relationship or job—or under the next rock! Our orientation is external. We explore new ways of behaving; we try on new lifestyles. We are excited one day, depressed the next. We are confused, uncertain, exuberant. We seek the solution that will solve our dilemma and make us ultimately happy.

We try two popular solutions that have been used for centuries—fight and flight.

Fight

We decide to stay put and make the best of the "slish" we're in. Hanging on, however, we chronically complain about our situation and wish again for the solution to appear. We race back to the security of the "old familiar spot." Back to our postponement games. Back to the life-cycle patterns of Stage I. We quit too soon, and eventually we're hounded by another triggering event yet more frightening than the last one.

Flight

We make a lifestyle or career change according to "the book" and go through all the outward motions. Inside nothing has changed, no new self-assessment has occurred, renewal has not been real, and we are once again stuck. There is a lot of outward activity, but no inner renewal.

We eventually come to the conclusion that there is no perfect solution. Like Band-Aids, the perfect solutions we counted on never quite solve the long-term problem. Band-Aids eventually fall off! Then we must seek the next solution, and the next, getting caught in a merry-go-round for long periods of time. The excursion process in this book will give you many skills to help you move from expecting a magic solution to the next stage of decision.

Stage V—A Decision for Renewal

Eventually, the quest for ultimate solutions loses its allure, and we seek resolution. Constant exploration and growth have sapped our energy. We seek relief. It's time to make a decision so we can stabilize and turn our attention to the other elements of our life that we have momentarily neglected. A decision is reached. Although perhaps it's not a perfect decision, we start from there.

Renewal: We recognize that *the* perfect solution does not exist, that life is a series of changes, each one moving us farther upward in the excursion spiral. As a result, we are more accepting of our experiences. We move ahead with our decisions, more confident of our own worth and confident about the future.

Stage VI—The Inventurous Life

When we decide to renew ourselves, we often get an awakening or a "blinding glimpse of the obvious." We see more clearly the purpose and meaning of our lives. "Aha! I have finally discovered the secret to life: there is no secret! Why didn't somebody explain that to me earlier?" As one thirty-three-year-old inventurer put it:

> The discovery is . . . I am on an excursion! Life is an upward spiral, a series of changes—the life spiral will end someday and I will die. If I keep growing, I live more fully. Life is a mystery to be lived, not an objective to be accomplished.

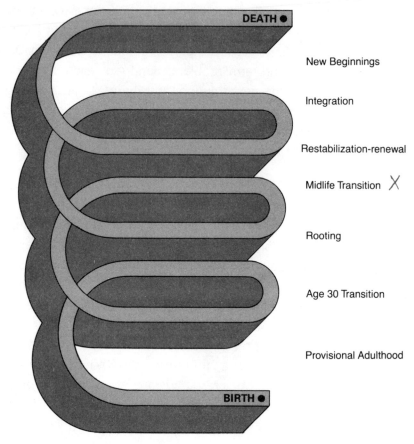

New Beginnings

Integration

Restabilization-renewal

Midlife Transition X

Rooting

Age 30 Transition

Provisional Adulthood

Figure 3.1. *The excursion model*

The inventurous life calls for plans, a map, and self-assessment. After all, you would not expect a person to design a complex building without a blueprint or after just a weeklong training program in architecture. Yet often we expect ourselves to be a different person—an inventurer, perhaps—from just reading a book like this. It is one thing to understand the inventurous life; it is quite another to map your own.

You are about to set out on one of the truly fun excursions of a lifetime—that of an inventurer. The model of the inventurer's life and the excursion process is the expanding spiral (figure 3.1). You have probably already seen it on your map and in various sections of the book. The spiral is many thousands of years old. The symbol originated in China to represent energy rising toward spiritual enlightenment. We have chosen to use the symbol to represent the blending of Eastern and Western thought and to reintroduce the ancient meanings of natural renewal and energy rising in a constant pattern of growth.

The Inventurous Life

The hypothesis of the inventurous life is that you continue growing, expanding, and getting better as you age—that you gain optimum balance and fuller functioning as a human being as you face crises, make choices, and find goals and objectives that have value and meaning for you. Purpose in life helps you to integrate imperfect solutions to career options.

Life Excursions

4   Adult Life Stages

Let's put our lives into a larger context by comparing them to what the researchers say is reasonable for us to expect in our lives and seeing how much we vary from person to person.

Recent research on the adult life cycle has given us a much better perspective for viewing life's changes—those we create and those imposed on us from the outside. The research findings so far are tentative. They are an attempt to explain the normal life patterns.

We know a great deal about how children grow and develop from birth through adolescence. Popular books remind us of the "terrible twos," the "fearless fours," the "noisy nines." But there still are few books that explain adequately the natural development of the adult. Adults presumably just emerge from their cocoons like butterflies at age twenty or so, ready to live rational, logical, steady existences. The notion was that whereas children grow in leaps and bounds, adults only age (until the seven-year itch, as folklore has it). Research conducted mostly on men's lives and reported by Levinson, Gould, Valliant, Sheehy, and others, shows that men experience predictable life stages, although each man has unique patterns, depending on his personality, life situation, cultural background, and life events.

There are also cycles within stages. Adulthood is a period of active and systematic change over one's lifetime. There seem to be special development tasks in each phase of life triggering "teachable moments" of peak readiness to move life forward.

Women's lives, however, are more difficult to predict. Iris Sangiuliano, in *In Her Time,* describes with vivid simplicity the dilemmas of the American women she spoke with.

> Woman, any woman, almost always leads a serial life. . . . Her life is never a straight line. Women's lives are bound by common threads. By and large, we postpone ourselves. We live a life derived from the male experience, whether we perceive the world through the kitchen window or the rungs of the corporate ladder. Woman invents herself around a man . . . intimacy precedes and postpones a separate identity.

Then how do women grow and develop?

> Most of us need to be transplanted . . . before we blossom. Simply, we grow and develop through contradiction and conflict and paradox. We grow, not through common, predictable transitions . . . but through the unpredictable events, those central critical events that dislodge and shock. How we perceive these shocks and what we do with them determines our development.

This may not be true for all women, of course, but it certainly holds true for many. Full-time career women may find themselves identifying with both male and female life-stage ideas, and feel confused as a result. Our own informal research shows that a continuing critical issue for women is balance between life and work, family and career, and that this is more intense and disquieting in the mid thirties.

The questions we will be asking you to reflect on as you read through this information are, "What life stage or life event do I most identify with at this time? And how is this affecting the rest of my life?"

The following is a brief outline of the stages of adult development with associated tasks for each stage. As you read them, remember that the ages we assigned to each stage are flexible: Some people experience the midlife reassessment earlier than thirty-nine, others later than forty-six, but most of us experience it some time. You may even experience the stages in a different order from that which we've described.

STAGES OF ADULTHOOD

Provisional Adulthood—22 to 28

During this stage you are building the first life system of your own and are making your first commitments to work, marriage and family, and other adult responsibilities. During provisional adulthood, you first put to use all of the parental upbringing, education, and advice that was part of the childhood and adolescent growth process. In the quest to answer the question "What do you do?" we try out the "shoulds" and "oughts" of our upbringing to reach for our own identity. Rarely analyzing commitments, it's a time to explore the real world of career, marriage, lifestyle.

Age Thirty Transition—29 to 32

During this transition stage, initial commitments to a life system are often reexamined and their meaning questioned. The surface bravado of the provisional period wavers as life begins to look more complex. Many times you will become impatient with the early choices made and will feel a new vitality springing from within to answer the question "What do I really want out of life?" Careers and marriages become particularly vulnerable to reassessment. Long-range implications of continuing with current career, community, and life system are challenged. In many people change will occur, and in many others there will be a renewed commitment and reaffirmation of their current career, life system, and community.

Rooting—33 to 38

After going through the age thirty transition, you will tend to buckle down tentatively to the life system that has been chosen, with a more definite attitude toward it. It is a time when you might seek a mentor— a patron or supporter to "show you the ropes."

Since so much of our identity is defined in terms of our work, we tend to spend a lot of our time working. In fact, there is often not enough time, it seems, for anything but work. Focused on money and career success, we try to make our mark through career achievement and hard work. In the midst of our striving we worry about becoming trapped, about others finding out I'm not as good as they thought I was, about messing up my personal and family life. Women feel stronger contradictory pulls than men during this time because this is a prime family time.

At some point, the time squeeze begins. Perhaps it is the first emotional awareness that death will come and that time is running out. You now want more than ever to be established.

When you start out on your career or family you establish certain goals and dreams. Some of these are attainable and desirable and others are not. This time squeeze during the rooting process begins to worry you. "Is there still time to change?" Uncertain about objectives and ambivalent about values, you need time to reassess. People frequently make major job or career changes in their late thirties because they think when they hit forty, it will be too late.

Midlife Transition—39 to 46

This is a period which for many has been labeled midcareer or midlife crisis. It is often a period of acute personal discomfort in which you may face the gap between youthful dreams and actual fulfillments. Likely limits of success and achievement in life and work become more apparent. There may be a difference between what you have reached and what you want. For some people, transition is merely a decade milestone. For others, however, it's a painful time of crisis. It's a lonely time, because each person is ultimately alone on the journey. You face the fact that you will die and that there are no guarantees. You look back on your life realizing you had no control over it really, and as you look ahead life frightens you.

Children are growing up and going away, and for many midlife adults, their own parents are now looking to them for support. They are "getting it from both ends." You will often ask many self-searching and spiritual questions in this period, such as "Why do I get up in the morning?" "What is my purpose?" "When am I having fun?" "Why can't I be accepted for what I am, not what 'they' [spouse, boss, society] expect me to be?" "Is it worth it to make it big?" In the search for answers that often consumes the midlife transition period, you may turn to a new career or other new directions in life. Many turn to counseling to get help.

There is no way to sail through this reassessment. It is deeper and harder than you have experienced before. And it is hard to describe to someone who has yet to experience it. Sometimes the only thing you know for sure is that you know nothing for sure.

Restabilization and Renewal—47 to 54

Once you've gone through the midlife transition satisfactorily, faced mortality, and forged a new life system, this stage might feel like the best time of life. Often unrushed by the sense of urgency of the thirties, people achieve a new stability. Adjusting to the realities of work, one may feel finally, "I have what I want. I feel secure enough to stop running and struggling. Work is no longer the single source of my identity. I'm not so concerned with what others think of me. It's easier to relax, open myself to new feelings, enjoy vacations." Launching children, adjusting to an empty nest, and handling increased demands of older parents are often tasks of this stage.

A career often takes on new meaning. Money becomes less important. Life is more stable because you listen more to the inner voice than to external demands. You may experience increasing attention to a few old values and a few friends. One hypothesis is that in this and the next stage, if you lose a spouse or close friend, you may go back into provisional-adulthood patterns, trying out life options all over again.

Many women are finding their new selves in this period and have renewed energy, which can be mystifying to their partners. It seems like a revolving door, with men coming in and women going out.

Integration—55 to 64

At this stage, people become more satisfied with themselves, coming to grips with what they have and haven't done. Delighted to see the vigor of life continuing, you often reengage with more energy in relationships, family, or community. Your concern is more with the "quality of life." You often feel a new tolerance for and companionship with your mate. A renewed focus on the spiritual dimension is also common. Eventually questions arise as to when to retire, what to do, and how to cope with sudden changes in lifestyle. It is a difficult step because nearly all of men's and many women's lives are attuned to work. Thus, an abrupt shift to leisure is often traumatic. The impact of this decision is compounded by aging, termination of longtime associations and friendships, and frequently a total lack of preparation.

New Beginnings—65+

Retirement is a stage that has been postponed—put out of mind—by both society and individuals. It cannot be postponed much longer. There are more Americans older than sixty-five at this moment than the sum of all Americans to have reached that age in the 212 years since the country was founded! No life stage line is sharper than the arbitrary one between those who are "active" and those who are "retired." Is retirement the best thing ever to happen? Or could it be the worst—the secret fear of many? An important step will be taken when preretirement planning includes more of the *reality* of retirement and less of its *mythology*.

For many people, the last third of life is a balance of play, continuing education, and work. But this work is often self-assigned, the work to which one had perhaps been drawn all one's life, the work one would do for nothing—the work of freedom. A goal and a purpose and a sense of achievement equal to, and perhaps surpassing, the goal and purpose of "career work" is a search for many. We need the models— the everyday heroes and heroines—of retirement to urge us on.

Some of the tasks after sixty-five include managing leisure time, seeking new achievement outlets, searching for meaning (claiming a legacy for one's life), reconciling one's spiritual nature, and being reconciled to death. We are just beginning to realize that if we don't understand retirement, we probably don't understand the rest of human existence either.

Using the excursion symbol as a representation of your life cycle (figure 3.1, p. 26), put an X on the spot that represents your position by age; mark an 0 on the spot you identify with emotionally.

 Enter your life stages in Box 2 on the Excursion Map on pages 188– 189. What stage do you identify most closely with? Pick a few key words to highlight those issues you identify most closely with.

WHO SHOULD I BE?

In our early life stages we spent so much of life asking that question over and over again. People asked, "What do you want to be?" We answered with one of our fantasies (professional football player, nurse, firefighter) or with answers that fit our families' expectations.

In early adulthood, the search continued, but the questions hit hard and fast. Whom do we want to marry? Do we want children? How many? Where do we want to live? To work? Often, answers came before we were ready.

As things settled into a pattern and we entered our thirties and forties, the old question arose again. What do we want? For some, the revival of that old question creates upheaval in their lives. They had been following society's dictated route without thinking where it might end.

Inventurers learned that the question is not "*What* do we want?" It is "*Who* are we and what do we need to help us be more completely who we are?"

5　Life-Cycle Review

Consider looking at your life events from the perspective introduced in the last chapter, the Excursion Model, the spiral that evolves ever upward, ever growing. Consider your life in relationship to your death. It's important to realize that this is sometimes a difficult and frightening thing to do, so proceed slowly and thoughtfully.

It is sometimes difficult to live a fully satisfying life until you have had a close personal awareness of your own death. The Indian poet Tagore states, "Death belongs to life as birth does. The walk is in the raising of the foot as in the laying of it down." People who can come to terms with their own deaths through physical or psychological experiences have found their lives profoundly altered as a result. For all of us, the last stage of our life cycle of growth is death.

The Excursion Model

Directions: The Excursion Model (figure 5.1) shows the relationship of your life to the general adult life stages, the ongoing excursions you experience from birth to death. Put your life into a different context.

1. Next to the death point, write the age you think you will be when you die and the year in which your death will occur.
2. Write the probable cause of your death.
3. Mark the approximate midpoint of your life. Write the age you will

be (were) at the midpoint. Mark the approximate place you are now. Write your present age next to it. How far along are you in your life? Halfway? Three fourths? One fourth?

4. Some people experience a definite time in their lives when they move from external expectations to internal considerations, a deepening and a move toward self-esteem. Draw a line cutting through the model at the place in which you decided to be in charge of your life, to take control and responsibility, to become an inventurer. If you have not done this yet, predict when you will.

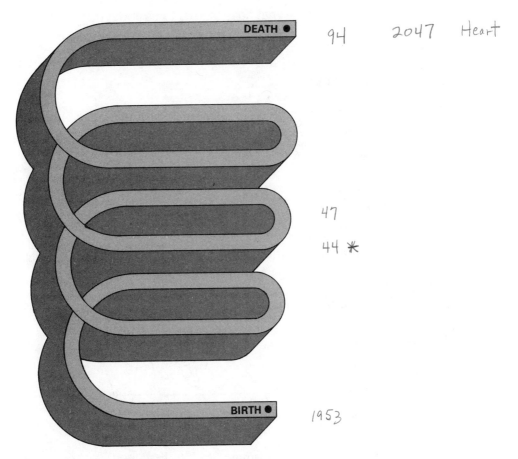

DEATH ●   94   2047   Heart

47

44 ✳

BIRTH ●   1953

Figure 5.1.   *The excursion model.*

LIFE EXCURSIONS

You will get a much more profound sense of yourself and the choices you have in your future if you have a better understanding of where you've been. There are themes and values that surface over and over again in our lives and wisdom is gained by acknowledging them and then either correcting them or embracing them. For instance, a theme of moving too fast from job to job so as to avoid finishing work projects can be changed when observed, and a different way of operating can be substituted. How do we find these themes and what do we do about them? What does this say to us about our future and inventuring? We'll explore these issues as we move into this Life Line Exercise.

Life Line

To begin exploring our lives we will complete our Life Line. The purpose of this exercise is to give us a view of our lives to date; the key events, both positive and negative, that have affected us.

On the grid below, record first the events you most recall in your life, and place a dot below or above the line, rating them as neutral, negative or positive (see sample). The farther below the line they appear, the more negative they were, and the farther above the line they are, the more positive they were for you. Connect your dots with a line chronologically so you can clearly see your Life Line.

Sample Life Line

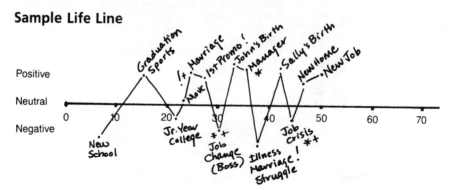

Your Life Line

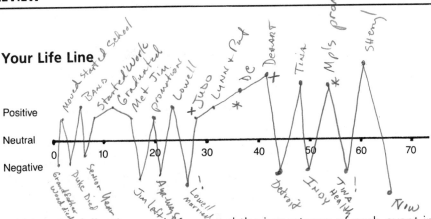

Using the following symbols, record the importance of each event in your life:

* * Places you took biggest risks
* \+ Best decisions ever made
* − Worst decisions ever made
* ! Experiences that molded or affected you the most

Write here the five life/work events that affected you most.

1. ___Ayr-Way___
2. ___Judo___
3. ___Lowell___
4. ___Tina___
5. ___Mpls.___

Questions for Reflection on the Life Line Exercise

Reflect on the exercise you have just completed. What are the themes or trends you see (or someone close to you sees) in your life? Answer these questions to see those trends or themes.

1. What caused your lows? Were they similar, such as work issues, relationship issues, health issues?
2. What do your five major life events consist of—work, health, family? Which personal relationships do you include in your life line? Which work events?
3. When did you take risks and what kind (financial, emotional, intellectual, physical)? Is there a pattern?

4. Is your line always above or below the neutral line? What does this tell you?

Now look more broadly at your Life Line and answer these questions quietly and sincerely.

5. What events caused you to learn the most about yourself? Why?
6. What was the most important question you were asking yourself ten years ago and what is the most important question you are asking yourself now? *Career*
7. How are you most different today from five years ago? *Health*
8. What are the biggest turning points in your life? Why?
9. How do you define and measure success? *work*
10. When you were at your lowest point, how did you cope? What does that tell you about your coping strengths? *work*
11. Who has most influenced your life (both positively and negatively)? Why?
12. What is the role of spirituality in your life? *Limited*
13. What are you afraid of facing? *Financial loss / stop growing*
14. From whom do you receive unconditional love in your life?

 Enter your life themes or insights from this exercise in Box 3 on the Excursion Map.

Reflect on what you've learned about yourself from these life-cycle review exercises and share as much as you care to with a friend, spouse, or colleague. You may wonder what other people learned from this experience. Here are a few examples:

- A thirty-year-old woman saw marriage as the low point emotionally on her Life Line—twice. She realized that her life was being determined by men she chose to marry for the wrong reasons. She wanted to develop herself professionally and make the care of the children a shared experience. Both of her husbands wanted her to be a wife and mother only, in return for financial security. She has determined now to consider *herself,* in addition to love, if she remarries.

- A forty-two-year-old man saw that each crisis in his life was followed by a positive experience. He decided to take more risks and "create crises" so he could experience more highs (move to a bigger city, ask for what he wanted, change jobs, travel without earning money first, hang glide).
- A fifty-year-old man found that all of his turning points involved close family members and social friends. Work had very little impact on his life. He decided to concentrate on lifestyle factors.
- A navy fighter pilot found that his life had been a series of distinct segments with abrupt endings. For instance, he was forced to retire at thirty-nine from an exciting, risky, and challenging life. He started all over with each new segment, and is emotionally exhausted as a result.
- A twenty-six-year-old teacher found her life line to be perfectly flat until she finished school and had to support herself. She felt that she was experiencing life for the first time.
- A man at the age of fifty-five realized that three quarters of his life was over. He'd never thought about it that way before. He decided to retire early and pursue his lucrative hobby.

Excursion Contract 2

We learn more completely when we share with someone else. Your goal is to highlight for someone what you learned from this exercise.

Share your insights in a way that helps you clarify and remember past experiences. You'll benefit and so will the person who listens to you.

1. With whom will you share this exercise?

_____   _____
Name   Phone

2. When?

_____   _____   _____
Date   Time   Place

3. What are the key insights you'll highlight?

_____

_____

_____

_____

_____

Discuss

- What were three "crossroads" in your life where your choice of paths made a major difference. List any paths you regret you did not travel.
- In "Ulysses," the poet Tennyson said, "I am part of all that I have met." The composite of all our life experiences weaves together into our own life's story. Some events, however, impact us more than others.—Review the five key experiences that have profoundly in"flu"enced your life/career directions.

6   Alone Together

Rarely will you find anyone who has been through a major life or career reassessment totally alone. There is always someone to read about, talk to, share feelings with, ask advice of, react to. But for each individual, the kinds and numbers of these people are different. When it comes right down to making decisions, making changes, starting to grow, *you* are still the only one who has control (even though you choose to abdicate it to others sometimes). It is the people around you, however, who can be the best catalysts, prodders, listeners, provokers, and models. Many people find that people around them are also obstacles, weights, discouragers, and martyrs. For serious inventurers, it is important to scrutinize your personal relationships—not scrap them, but cultivate people who will be supportive during the change. For many people, this means some new friends.

One of your best supporters, of course, could be you! Unfortunately, many of us rarely take the time even to get to know ourselves in simple ways such as journal writing, trips alone, or even walks alone. In Outward Bound Life and Career Renewal groups, individuals spend twenty-four hours on a "solo," alone in the wilderness, listening, thinking, writing. Some people say that it takes up to fifteen hours just to get the ringing city noise out of their ears. Then they can begin to hear the wilderness sounds much better. If you have never been on a "solo" experience, plan now to take some time (two hours, an afternoon, a day, a weekend) to be by yourself. You could start by eating out or going to a park, another town, the woods, or across the country. This can be a very exhilarating experience. At first, a lot of fears and other buried feelings may emerge. Start with small increments of time and more structured activities. It can be even more significant if you record your reactions.

INVENTURE NETWORK

There are three major categories of people who will be useful to you on your inventure. You will need all of them sometime during the trip, and some of them will be major forces in your life. The three groups together are called an inventure network (figure 6.1). Let's take each of these categories of people separately, define them, and look at how other people have used each of them in their excursions.

Role Models

These people fit the image of what you'd like to be. They may not even know you, but you identify with some characteristics that you like in them. They represent a standard you are aiming for that will help you set goals and mark progress. We generally use models for change in two steps. First, we recognize what qualities in that person we like or want; second, we imagine or imitate the behavior in our minds.

Many people will not make changes in their lives until they can "see" themselves in the new image. They must imagine themselves speaking in front of a group, finishing school, winning a race, not smoking, hitting a golf ball. Until they can accept themselves in the new image, they won't change. Role models, or respected images, are important in forming the new behavior that you want to cultivate, and for many they are the first step toward change.

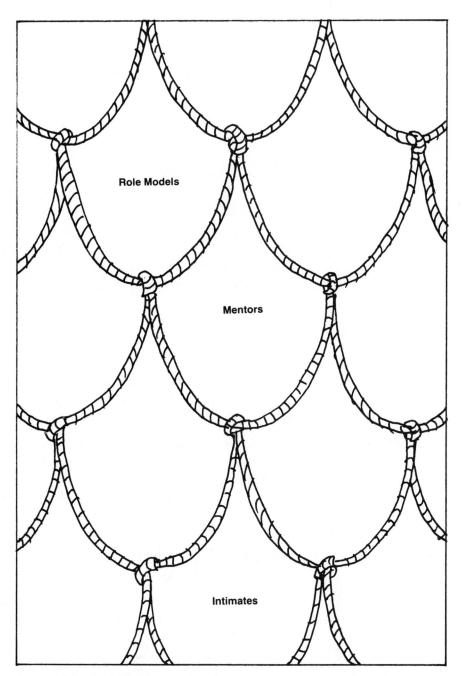

Figure 6.1. *The inventure network*

CASE STUDY

Frank had a difficult time speaking smoothly before a group of people. He had all the organizational skills, but he just panicked before he was about to go on. He observed a very accomplished speaker carefully to see how he started his speech, what he did with his hands and his facial expressions, how he "read" the audience. Then, right before his next speech, Frank went to the large room where the meeting was to be held and imagined himself as the man he had observed. He imagined what the audience would be like. He went to the podium and stood behind it, looking out over the imagined audience. Finally, he rehearsed the whole scene in his head and spoke out loud occasionally, just to hear himself. He finished the speech and anticipated the response. Then he made any changes that had occurred to him during rehearsal. The next day, he had the experience of a lifetime. The speech went exceptionally well—after all, it was the second time he had given it to the same audience!

Think of people (alive or dead) whom you consider role models— people having some characteristics or qualities (personal, intellectual, athletic, spiritual, emotional) you'd like to imitate. Your role models can be friends, teachers, novelists, sports heroes, spouses, parents, historical figures. Enter the names of your role models in the appropriate spaces on the personal inventure network in figure 6.2.

Mentors

Mentors have been described as "what most people are missing in their life excursions." We used to think only women and minorities lacked mentors. Now we know that *most* people cannot identify their mentors. The questions then arise: What are mentors? Where do you find one?

Mentors are people you consider wise and trustworthy individuals, those who serve as your advisers, guides, or counselors in helping you fulfill your potential. The term "mentor" comes from a Greek legend

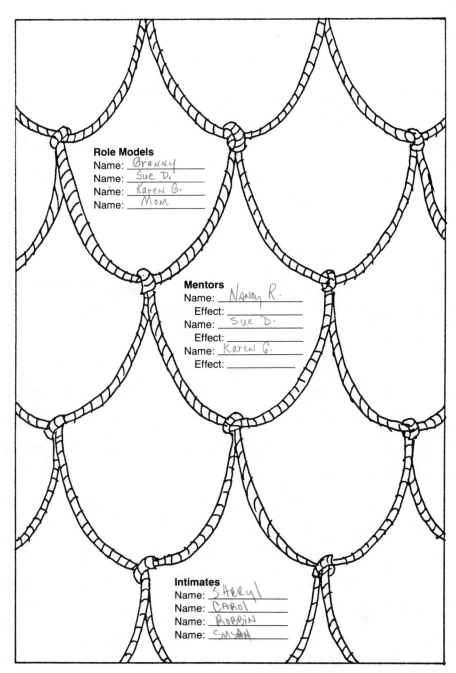

Figure 6.2. Your personal inventure network

about Mentor, a friend and adviser of Odysseus and a guardian of his son. Mentor's role was to motivate others and help them accomplish their goals.

Mentors first and foremost are good listeners. They can wear a number of hats in relation to your excursion. Mentors, like role models, can be colleagues, teachers, religious leaders, friends, relatives, spouses, social acquaintances, or supervisors. Their main role is to help you to reflect, grow, wait, change, or do whatever you need to do to reach your personal or professional potential.

Mentors can be recognized by the things they do (or by the things you want them to do):

- They listen.
- They ask questions.
- They help you develop your plans further.
- They influence, but don't determine, your plans.
- They help you solve problems.
- They expect you to use your own best judgment.
- They help you find your own skills and potential.
- They do not expect you to be "just like they are."
- They challenge and prod you.
- They support and trust you.
- They give you advice on technical or organizational matters, serving as expert resources.
- They share your ups and downs.
- They provide you with realistic personal information.

Mentors can be cultivated—and sometimes have to be. Few people have thought seriously of having a mentor. Fewer yet have thought about acting as a mentor to someone else. So there may be a mentor in your life that you just don't recognize as such. Or you may realize that you don't have a mentor. Now is the time to look for a person who can fulfill some of the expectations listed above. It may take time and some effort, but it's well worth it. People who have successfully made lifestyle or career changes say that at crucial times, the people around them, including mentors, made an enormous difference in their outlook and on their persistence.

CASE STUDY

Jane had wanted to start her own private counseling practice for a whole year. She had been working as a counselor (psychologist) in a treatment center for six years and had gained enough experience and a good enough reputation to work on her own. She knew the overhead costs, start-up costs, the principles she'd use, and even the professional referrals she could count on for clients. But there was something missing—action. Every few months she met with a long-term friend, an older, more experienced person in another profession, to share ideas and digest new insights. At their meeting, he asked her about her work and she replied, "I need a place to work and my first client." He said, "If I can help you find a place, can you get the clients?" Needless to say, she started her private practice on a part-time basis within six weeks.

CASE STUDY

Bill was really getting bored by the kinds of skills he was using on his job within a large foods firm. After four years, he'd got the job so well refined that he could do it without feeling challenged. He talked with a colleague from another company who had recently made a job shift within that company. They went over his skills, abilities, and interests and decided which directions he could go in. He wanted to work as part of a team developing a new product within his division. He was excited about the prospects and talked to his supervisor about it. His balloon burst. His supervisor didn't see any possibilities like that at the present time, although he really agreed with Bill's assessment and proposal. Bill decided not to give up and went back to his colleague to plan the next steps. He decided to talk informally to other people at work about his ideas. After many conversations over a period of weeks, he was getting discouraged. One day at lunch he saw an old colleague from another department, and they began to share ideas. The projects he was interested in were actually being started in another place within the company. He knew immediately that his opportunity had come. He worked for weeks with his supervisor and the other department head arranging for a transfer. It worked, and in time he was doing what he wanted to do—and was a much happier man.

CASE STUDY

Jean had been at home raising three small children for the first twelve years of her marriage. Her youngest was in school now, and she had a lot of time on her hands. At church one Sunday, she just happened to mention her dilemma to an older friend who explained, "That's exactly how I felt when my kids went to school, but I didn't do anything about it for years!" As they talked, it dawned on Jean that she really wanted to return to school to finish her B.A. degree. Her friend knew several people involved with local adult-oriented college programs and served as a source of referral and support for the next six months. Jean put together an art and counseling program that she'd been thinking about for years as a result of her community experiences with adolescent drop-in centers. Her mentor continued to encourage her, and their friendship grew at the same time. They may eventually start a small pilot art program for youth at their church.

Now it's time for you to consider your own mentors. Remember, mentors can be community leaders, colleagues, or supervisors who are interested in your growth and will encourage and push you; they can be experts in an area who can provide you with information or direction; or they can be other people who are just willing to listen, share, support, advise, and guide. They should be people you trust and respect. Your needs for mentors will change. You may have a mentor and be a mentor at the same time. If you don't have a mentor, here are some suggestions for finding one.

1. Go to professional meetings. Consider your professional colleagues.
2. Talk to speakers at conferences.

3. Cultivate teachers.
4. Look over your holiday card list for "sleepers" among people you already know.
5. Think of people at work whom you respect and enjoy talking to.
6. Consider community colleagues, political friends, PTA members, musical group members, church affiliates, committee members, club members, civic group members, arts organization members.
7. Don't overlook sports partners.
8. Use impersonal sources such as novelists and columnists.
9. Consider family members—brothers, sisters, aunts, uncles, parents.
10. Always be alert in new situations. Mentors lurk in the most unsuspecting places—airports, supermarkets, barbershops.

Enter the names of your mentors and what effects each has on you in the appropriate network space in figure 6.2, page 49.

Intimates

Intimates are a very special part of your inventure network; they are your closest, warmest, truest, and most important friends. They stick with you "no matter how tough the going gets." It isn't always easy for them to be around when you are going through changes, especially when it seems as though you'll never get out of limbo; but remember, they're around for the celebrations too. You can share anything with these people and not be afraid or embarrassed. You can trust and depend on them—because they care about you.

Usually this group of people is quite small—spouse, partner, best friend, neighbor, or relative. Many people realize that even though they have friends or may live with someone, they have few, if any, intimates. Others think they have ten or more—only because they share their feelings freely. Most men, until recently, have thought of their intimates as their wives, lovers, or sports partners—by titles rather than by their roles as people who have shared their innermost dreams, fears, and accomplishments. Increasingly, men have allowed themselves the experience of sharing feelings, ideas, hopes, and laughter with intimates.

Intimates are not necessarily people with whom you share sexual experiences, but rather people of both sexes with whom you share vulnerability and closeness. Intimates, too, can be cultivated—and must be attended to for the relationship to grow. Entire books have been written about the care and feeding of intimate relationships.

The closer the relationship is and the more important it is, the more difficult it is to establish. Most good relationships cannot be pushed—they have to evolve over time. You usually can't just walk up to someone and ask that person to be your intimate. Just being aware of the need for intimates will be the first step. People still go out to "look for dates, find their catch, fill a void." The irony of the situation is that until you look within and develop your own personal lifestyle, you won't be the kind of person who would attract the kind of person you want anyway. It's all got to start from the inside out.

If you have no intimates, mentors and friends can provide some closeness for the time being. You can be more aware of your interest in cultivating a deeper friendship. You may be a person who says you don't need intimates. That's possible. If you want to make any significant changes in your life or your work, however, intimates for support and encouragement are often the factor that makes the difference. Families or intimates are often profoundly affected by the changes you make, and it is crucial to let them in on your excursions at appropriate times. They will experience many of the feelings you do in the consideration of change, and if you can get their assistance and support, it may be the most enriching experience of your lives.

Here are some suggestions from other inventurers for ways to involve your intimates in the process:

- Share the book with them and have everyone do the exercises, discussing them at specific times.
- Take a long weekend together away from home to discuss life plans and work options.
- Take turns making changes, supporting each other.

- Start a book club, choosing books on change and growth.
- Form an inventurer's support group with friends, church members, and neighbors to encourage one another in your endeavors.
- Discuss these exercises with young people in their youth groups (teams, scouts, church groups) and get them to share their sentiments.
- Go to a family counselor to get an objective view of your decision-making processes.
- Go slowly—all people fear change when it may have an impact on them.

There will be a category of friends, acquaintances, and relatives who will not be listed in any of the categories of role models, mentors, intimates. They are fine friends and comrades, but will not be as crucial in your excursion. Don't forget them, but don't concentrate all your time on them! Also, some categories may overlap; some mentors may be intimates, and some role models may be mentors.

Write the names of intimates in the appropriate network space in figure 6.2.

   Enter names of your best role model, best mentor, and closest intimate in Box 4 of your Excursion Map.

You can't get by with just identifying the people in your inventure network; you must make use of them to get maximum benefit. You may already be doing this, but follow along anyway.

THE DIALOGUE

Invite one of your inventure network members who is a good listener to meet with you to start some exploration. It may be the first time you've sat down with anyone just to talk about yourself, and that's what you are about to do.

1. Actually hand over this book and have the person read the statements in this dialogue exercise to you one at a time. You may want to look

over the list first and think through the responses briefly before sharing them.

2. Finish the sentences out loud, and have your partner jot down the answers in the space provided.

3. Do not get into conversations about how the other person would complete the sentences. It's your turn this time.

4. When you're finished, look over your answers for any themes, recurrent ideas or qualities, any new insights. Write them in the space provided, for example, "Every time I dream about the future, I'm involved in sports" or "I'm definitely not using my best skills, the ones others recognize in me" or "I'm frustrated!"

5. Let your partner then comment.

6. If you'd like, switch roles and ask the questions of the other person.

The Dialogue Questions

1. Five words that describe my personality best are (*not* roles such as worker, wife, teacher):

   Energetic   *Outgoing*
   High Standards   *Cautious*
   Caring   *Assertive*

2. Two feelings I never allow myself to express to others are:

   Fear
   Anger

3. The main, overriding concern or challenge at this stage in my life is:

   What do I want to be when I grow up.

4. In the midst of a triggering event, I would feel most comfortable talking to: Sheryl

5. My best childhood memory is: Granny's 80th Birthday

6. My definition of success is: Being the best at what you are doing & being happy doing it

7. Two perceptions of me that I don't like are:

Hard-Ass

Hard to get to know

8. The type of people I like best are:

Honest
Open Minded

9. Ways I have fun are:

Playing outdoors
Music

10. Three occupations I can fantasize myself doing are:

Farmer   Teacher
Doctor

11. If I had $3000 extra for the month, I would:

Travel somewhere I haven't been

12. If I were to choose an object or concept to describe myself, it would be a (kind of car—silver Datsun, yellow VW, gold Cadillac, blue jeep; kind of weather—sunny, cloudy, stormy, hot and muggy), because: *Sunset - Always Changing*

13. Four things I dream of doing before I die are:
Building house on farm
Spending time family
Taking Mom Nigura Falls *Black Belt*
Getting my 6th Degree

14. Two different places I can imagine myself wanting to live are:
Ky /IND

15. The way I've changed most in the last five years is:
Less trusting

16. The person whose life I most admire is:
Granny

17. A good question for a mentor to ask me would be:

Write down any themes, insights, recurring ideas, or qualities (have your partner help you if you like).
Family
Location
Job

➡ Enter your major dialogue insights in Box 5 on your Excursion Map.

Lifestyles

7 The Balancing Act

L ifestyle is simply how you choose to live your life, including all of life's components; health, work, family and social relationships, spiritual dimensions, community. The theme we hear over and over pertaining to lifestyle is balance. Most of us are out of balance, and some of us are falling apart as a result.

Dividing our lives into three sectors called <u>body, mind, and spirit</u> is one way to think about balance in relation to lifestyle. We could use the categories of work, leisure, family; or work, social, and personal relationships; but we think categories of body, mind, and spirit are broader and will be intriguing to think about.

In our discussion of lifestyle we will consistently mention three factors—key ingredients—that must be in relative balance for a full and satisfying life. The three elements are the intellectual (mind), the physical (body), and the emotional (spirit) as shown in figure 7.1. If these three elements are in balance, they reinforce one another, for example, good physical health encourages clearer thinking. If they are out of balance, they multiply problems, for example, when you have the flu, it is hard to pick yourself up and get involved in a tough task at work.

The areas of overlap, or integration, among mind, body and spirit are important to recognize. Each has an influence on the others, and failure to realize this can have negative effects, for example, trying to push yourself to write a paper or complete a project when you are emotionally exhausted. The three factors multiply their positive effects when they

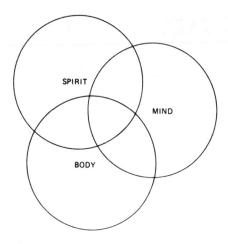

Figure 7.1.   *Three key ingredients of lifestyle*

Figure 7.2.   *Three key elements of sailing*

are in balance. Increasingly, we are learning how much control the mind and spirit can have over the body from studying psychosomatic illnesses and the effect of meditation on the body among other things..

A simple analogy would be to liken the three factors to sailing a sailboat (see figure 7.2).

The mind: There has to be a sailor or someone to control and steer
(*the sailor*)   the boat. The person who holds the rudder and the
                       ropes determines the direction and the speed. In your
                       life, your mind is the element that controls your func-
                       tioning.

The body: The obvious physical structure of the boat, the hull and
(*the hull*)   mast, are like your physical body. People can determine
                       the type of boat from the structure. In your life, your
                       physical structure and the way you care for it determine
                       how you are seen by others.

The spirit: The sails, which catch the wind and enable the boat to
(*the sails*)   move, are like your spirit—sometimes mysterious, other
                       times cooperative, other times flapping in the breeze. In

your life, your spirit gives you inner strength to change and grow and often has the strongest effect on your growth.

We need all three in order to move about successfully, but the movement toward some goal seems to be determined primarily by the sailor. However, the working together of all elements is necessary. The sailor depends on the sails filling and the structure being well designed.

Let's try to describe the lifestyle integration of the three factors more clearly. We can first define the factors as follows:

1. *Intellectual*. Activity and interest related to the mind—reading, learning, verbal communication, thinking, organizational skill, writing, creativity, intuition.
2. *Physical*. Activities and interest related to the body—exercise and health, strength, energy, food and nutrition, outward appearance (clothes, hair, cosmetics), physical structures, and spaces you live in.
3. *Emotional*. Activities and interests related to the spirit—feelings, attitudes, values, personal esteem, relationships with others, and spirituality of all kinds.

Each lifestyle factor has the potential to be positive and growth-producing. But there is a danger in overfocusing on any one area to the detriment of the others. You might get out of balance. You might lose perspective.

What happens if you live out of balance or with one area very diminished for long periods of time? During that time, you feel incomplete as a person, and eventually you might suffer from the imbalance. People who use one area only (of the three) or almost exclusively are usually addicted. Here are some examples of common lifestyle imbalances:

1. *Mind supreme*. These very unemotional, unspontaneous people live in such an intellectual, work-oriented world that there is little fun in life. They are frightened of people and situations unless they can control them rationally. They scoff at things that are a waste of time,

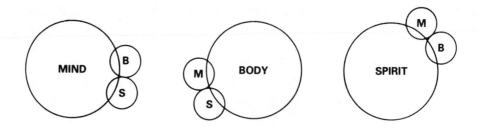

such as playing. They are frequently addicted to work or to ideals.

2. *Body supreme*. These people are expert at looking good and/or persistent in doing exceptionally well at physical activities. Physical appearance or physical prowess is of primary interest. These people's lives are geared toward appearances, and they are often immature intellectually and emotionally after initial contact. They are happy only during a physical chase or challenge. As they age, they get more and more frantic. They are frequently addicted to exercise, physical attractiveness, or sex.

3. *Spirit supreme*. Expert at emotion, these people are often unstable and unpredictable. Their turbulent emotions rule. They feel from moment to moment and direct their lives on the basis of whims, moving from one high to the next. They seek quick solutions to increase the effect—relationships, mind-altering chemicals, creative expression, spirituality. Their self-esteem is often low because environmental happenings dictate their self-images. They tend to get swallowed up personally in events, only to emerge with less and less ability to resolve things rationally. They begin to wonder about their ability to think at all. They are frequently mentally or emotionally ill, chemically dependent, or addicted to any variety of things or people (food, relationships, money).

When we go on for long periods of time without acknowledging our addicted behavior, we may even experience a total separation of the circles. When this happens, there is no way for one part of us to give messages to the other parts and we are in jeopardy. Excessive negative behavior usually results, even suicide.

Throughout your life, there will be times when you will have to focus on one area of your three life factors. Any triggering event can cause your circles to be way out of balance, as can a certain phase of your life. Review the adult life stages mentioned in chapter 4. At a time of reassessment—age thirty transition, for example—you may temporarily focus on the spirit factor, looking inward at values and beliefs, at spiritual ideals. When you are through the transition, your three factors come into better balance again, and you can throw yourself into home, work, and other activities with more intellectual and physical energy. Another example is midlife transition, when physical and emotional issues loom large. You may lean heavily in those directions for a while (feeling at times that it'll never be over!), and one day it all looks as though it's back in perspective.

When one of your life factors is out of proportion, the common reaction is to put emphasis only on the swollen circle to get it back into proportion and become comfortable again. This causes more stress on that circle and can compound the original problem. It can cause you to wallow in the stress. An example would be someone who is injured in an athletic event and pushes the healing process too quickly, thus increasing the likelihood of further injury, or a person who tries to get over a death by getting very busy, denying the emotions, thus putting *more* emphasis on them.

A more effective way to cope with a swollen circle would be to put emphasis on the other two circles, this increasing their size and getting

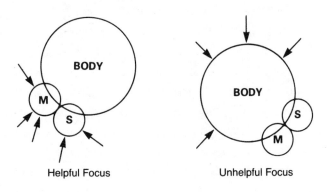

Helpful Focus   Unhelpful Focus

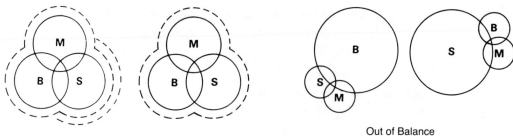

Inventurer's Choices   Out of Balance

more balance. Using the above example, the injured person could exercise to heal appropriately, and focus on the ways in which these other circles could be enlarged. They might include reading, mind games, or journal writing for the mind, or music, humor, and friendships for the spirit. The body needs time to heal. The person experiencing a death can begin adding other activities gradually, while writing in a journal about the loss, getting enough sleep, and making sure to exercise and eat well.

Inventurers have developed their coping techniques and know how to use them when necessary. They still experience stress but they know how to get themselves back into relative balance when they need to. You'll have a chance at the end of the lifestyle section to learn how to do that too. Inventurers choose at various times to deliberately stretch the walls of their circles, push themselves to grow, to change, to get out of balance. That's how they thrive. And if a triggering event ever should come along, they revert to their tried and true coping techniques to get back in some semblance of balance. We are rarely totally in balance and that is fine. We do not strive for perfection.

In this section, you will complete exercises dealing with each lifestyle factor. If you are not satisfied with a factor and you want some change, you can decide to make changes. Don't read through the section and say it won't work without working on it. That is like letting someone else decide for you that you can't change. *You* are the one who makes it work.

Are you ready to go? First, find a quiet, comfortable place away from the usual distractions. Give yourself enough time to do some writing as well as some reflection. Plan several sessions to complete the chapters in this section.

LIFESTYLE BALANCE

Start the whole process with a self-diagnosis. Draw the size of circle that represents the amount of activity of each life factor for you (body, mind, spirit). Are you completely oriented to one over the others; for instance, do you let your mind rule, always analyzing and arguing about terms, definitions, strategies and outcomes? Or have you been at home with small children, concentrating your communication on nonverbal areas for so many years that your spirit circle is large and the others smaller? Or are you such a health fanatic that your body circle is crowding out the people in your life? Give an overall impression, not a complicated analysis (you can do that later). If you are way out of balance, do you know why? Being continually way out of balance may even begin to seem comfortable for us, but we are negating parts of ourselves and sooner or later we will feel the effects.

My Life Balance

(Draw your circles here.)

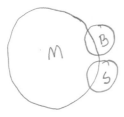

▬▬▶   Draw a set of circles in Box 6 on your Excursion Map.

8   Body

The body is the physical factor in the three life factors. Your body is your primary way of experiencing the world you live in. Just as the body of a boat that is well taken care of performs better, so, too, inventurers realize that physical well-being is essential to the excursions they undertake. To consider new options, to venture and explore, requires optimum health and energy.

Inventuring is a term that embodies new expectations of health and well-being. To inventure means to recognize that you do have choices and this recognition carries with it the willingness to live with the consequences of those choices.

For example, in order to complete a big work project you may place yourself under unusual stress, forget to exercise, neglect your diet. These are your choices. If such choices are occasional, you'll probably handle the stress just fine. But when such conditions are prolonged they might result in tired muscles, sore throat, and a congested head, sending you to bed. Are you responsible for the cold? Yes, of course, at some level you are. You didn't create the virus, but you made yourself vulnerable to its visit. An inventurer will generally accept the cold as an important message from the body and use it as a chance to rest and rebalance.

We learn time and time again that illness, pain, and accident can alert us to deeper needs that are going unmet. Our bodies are constantly trying to tell us something. But many of us simply don't listen to its messages.

Illnesses and symptoms are often not really the problem. They are actually the body's attempt to solve a problem. It is important to look below the surface to address the real needs.

It is very important to be aware that the body is a tool and not the entire self. The body is a support system for the mind and spirit; thus, it is necessary to take care of it. If the body is constantly sick the mind is absorbed by pain and is not free to think about other things.

Inventurers are aware that a key question is "How can I maintain a positive relationship with my body so that my purpose in life can be carried out?" The inventuring process blends mind, body, and spirit to carry out one's purpose in life.

LIFESTYLE

The key is lifestyle—the range of choices under your control such as how you eat, exercise, relax, manage stress and in general treat your body. Environment is important, and heredity plays a key role, but only lifestyle is under your direct influence.

Your Lifestyle

List some things that come to mind when you think of your own physical lifestyle.

What would I like to eliminate, do less of, or use less of to be more healthy?	What would I like to do more of, or use more of in order to be more healthy?
Remove stress Eat Right Loose weight	Exercise Take vitamins

Lifestyles are unique to each person. No expert can tell you what to do or how to do it. If you are to become more healthy you need to start listening to your body, then provide it with the best lifestyle conditions so that it can heal itself. Only the body heals itself.

The contribution of our values, our sense of meaning, and our purpose in life to our health can no longer be denied as critical factors. Health comes when we have achieved a level of integration among the mind, the body, and the spirit; when we allow ourselves to be in balance.

The inventuring process recognizes that the body dimension has many important factors: self-responsibility, nutritional awareness, fitness, play, stress management, and environmental sensitivity. This chapter is designed to get you moving, to help you in self-evaluation, in the awareness of what is working or not working in your body dimension. It is not an in-depth chapter on "wellness." There are many excellent resources for you to use, to educate and challenge yourself further in this area, including:

The Wellness Workbook, by Regina Ryan and Dr. John Travis
14 Days to a Wellness Lifestyle, by Dr. Don Ardell
The Well Body Book, by Hal Bennett and Mike Samuels
Medical Self-Care, by Dr. Tom Ferguson

The inventuring process extends the definition of health to encompass awareness, choices and growth. Inventurers realize they don't just get well or stay well. There are many levels of wellness just as there are levels of illness. Nor is wellness simply the absence of disease. Wellness is not a static state.

A "well" person is not necessarily the strongest, the fittest or the prettiest or even the illness-free person. You can be living a wellness lifestyle and yet be physically handicapped, aged, in the midst of a triggering event, in pain, plateaued, or unemployed.

Most people think of body health as a state when you are "not sick." Health is associated with the absence of something—illness. When you believe that, the best you can hope for is not to be sick.

Inventurers describe health as a positive dimension. The idea of inventuring is to "promote" health—beyond being "not sick." There is a great deal more to health than absence of illness.

Let's explore areas of the body dimension that promote health beyond the absence of illness.

Energy Style

Often, we experience an "energy crisis"—a human energy crisis—when we have to choose how to expend our energies during the 168 hours we have to live each week. We lament, "I wish there was more time to get everything done!" But that's it—168 hours is all!

How can you deal with the frustration of not having enough time to get things done? The first step is to be aware of the way you are using your energy. Our society has given very little attention to the importance of balance. Some of us have a work ethic which views a person who takes time off as being unproductive and lazy, yet balance is needed even more today because of the pace of "present shock."

Energy styles are just emerging as an area of study. The problem at this point is figuring out the influence that energy has on our lives and what, if anything, we want to do about it.

Everyone's energy needs are different. Our energy patterns are determined primarily by social patterns: job, television schedules, family responsibilities. Some people feel best going to bed early, getting a full night's sleep, and awakening early in the morning. Others feel best if they sleep during the day and spend their working hours at night. Some people attempt to conform to the eight-hour standard for sleep; others feel best with four to five hours. Everyone has a personal energy style, and it is helpful to be sensitive to it. Your body actually gives you messages, if you will listen. The amount of energy you have available for activities during a day and the amount of "recreation" you need will be highly individualized.

As a group, physical laborers are more in touch with their energy styles than are office workers, professional people, and homemakers.

Fatigue in people who use their bodies in their work is more straight-forward and easier to "read." Mental or nervous fatigue is more subtle and indirect. Mental and emotional efforts require as much energy as does physical work, but different parts of your body are doing the work. Complete the following exercises to learn more about your energy expenditure and preferences.

Energy Expenditure

Rate your energy expenditure below.

1. Rate yourself in column 1 on a continuum of 1 to 3, with 1 indicating a very low level of energy expenditure and 3 a very high level. "I think about my job all the time" would be 3; "I don't feel I spend enough time with my children" would be 1.

2. In column 2, rate your *preference*, the way you want to distribute your energy, with a score of 3 being for the person or activity you want to expend most energy on, and a score of 1 for the activities on which you want to expend the least. Are you comfortable with the way you are distributing energy now?

	1. Energy expenditure			2. Energy preferences		
Career	1	2	③	1	②	3
Friends	①	2	3	1	②	3
Social	①	2	3	1	②	3
Spouse/significant other	1	②	3	1	2	③
Children	1	2	3	1	2	3
Sports	①	2	3	1	②	3
Hobbies	①	2	3	1	②	3
Self-growth	①	2	3	1	2	③
Community service	①	2	3	1	②	3
Personal time	①	2	3	1	②	3
Spirituality	①	2	3	1	2	③
Adventure	①	2	3	1	2	③

3. In summary list those areas in which you would definitely like to spend more time and those to which you would devote considerably less time.

More time	Less time
Family	Career
Self-growth	
Spirituality	
Adventure	

PLAY

Defining your philosophy about enjoyment of life is an essential step toward improving and maintaining a high quality of life.

Play is a primary life activity. There's nothing more characteristic of children than their love of play. But play can be more difficult than work for adults!

What happens to play as we grow older?

As adults, we often look at play as serving some utilitarian purpose— losing weight, reducing stress, or training for a sport. For many of us, physical education classes had the opposite effect from the desired one, turning what was play into duty, pleasure into work.

There are many ways we can enjoy ourselves, and often with little cost. There's no reason why you shouldn't have fun in the process of living.

Play influences the rest of what we do and how we do it. Our health is affected by our level of playfulness, as is the process of aging.

Woody Allen said, "Most of the time I don't have much fun. The rest of the time I don't have any fun at all."

Playfulness is the heart of alive lifestyles and relationships. As we mature, we sometimes lose the ability to laugh—particularly at ourselves!

Yet play is a primary life category and laughter is great medicine: "She who laughs . . . lasts!" Play and laughter dissolve tension, keep things in perspective. Most of us need to remind ourselves to "lighten up!"

Many of us are at a loss when it comes to fun because we haven't had it for so long, or we think that what others do for fun isn't fun for us. One definition for <u>fun</u> might be "<u>an activity (usually unpaid) that relaxes you, is not on your list of 'to dos,' and takes your mind completely away from your troubles and your work.</u>" Listed here are a few activities that other people have mentioned. Yours may be very different.

Gardening	Reading	Sailing
Card playing	Watching TV	Remodeling
Dancing	Traveling	Collecting
Outdoor sports	Eating	Bird watching
Crafts	Cooking and baking	Studying and research
Puzzles	Sewing	Geneology
Games	Home projects	Fine arts
Sex	Car repair	Quilting
Massages	Walking and hiking	Socializing
Writing	Camping	

Are We Having Fun Yet?

Step 1:   Think of something funny that happened to you recently, the crazier the better! Jot it down, then tell it to a friend.

Video Conf w/ GM's echoing

Step 2:   What can you do to bring more fun and laughter into your life? Your marriage? Write down your ideas and discuss them with your partner.

Step 3: List the five ways you really have fun. Jot the date you last did each of them.

Boating — 8/97

Judo — 3 years ago

Camping — Last Summer

Friends —

Farm

Step 4: Which people bring the most play and sparkle into your life? Which people do you purely "enjoy" being with the most? Are there others whom you really don't enjoy but who take up much of your time? Do you want to do anything to change this?

Family / Friends

TRIGGERING EVENTS AND TENSION

We always wish we could do away with our tensions. You often hear "If I just didn't have to work under so much pressure, I could relax and enjoy my life more, but the competition these days. . . ."

Jobs are never tense; people are. Coping with our self-induced tension is a vital skill. If we were completely free of all tension, we would no longer be alive. But there is positive tension and negative tension. Some tension is useful and productive; other tension gets in our way and inhibits us from performing as effectively as we might. There is not always a sharp dividing line between the positive and negative tensions. Too much negative tension can exact a physical as well as an emotional toll. Current research, pioneered by Dr. Hans Selye, a Canadian physician, links ailments such as ulcers, colitis, headaches, backaches, heart attacks, cancer, diabetes, and arthritis to stress. It also appears that chemical substances secreted into our bloodstreams in excess when we are experiencing stress have the effect of lowering our resistance to contagious or infectious illnesses. We are more likely to catch the flu or colds during a period of life stress than when the body's response to pressure is at a more positive level.

How much tension is too much? It depends on your ability to cope. Your answer is directly related to your evaluation of the forces or pressures influencing your behavior. Tension stems from within you—your reactions to external events.

How hard should I work? You'll have to answer another question first: "What do I want from my life?" But even that isn't the most basic question. The question "How hard should I work?" boils down to some fundamental choices about the way you want to live. How big a family, mortgage, or ego do you have to support?

Tension is a very real fact of life in our day-to-day activities. Each of us confronts the press of time, decision making, competition, and keeping up communications in relationships. In each case, it is not the "triggering event" itself that causes stress; rather, it is our response to that kind of situation. The vital element in coping with tension is the acceptance of the fact that no one outside of yourself can cause your tension. If you are tense, it's because you do it to yourself! Of course, there is a temptation to play "victim"—to feel that life would be much easier or that we would be much less tense if *they* would shape up. However, in any tension situation, you have two primary choices: (1) change the situation; or (2) change your mindset about the situation.

Three positive choices for managing triggering events and tension are

1. Learn to be still.
2. Learn to relax.
3. Learn to create a positive environment.

Be Still

The stress of living today requires daily safety valves to keep us healthy and happy. Everyone needs a period of mental and physical solitude daily.

Many of us simply don't listen to ourselves. We're so busy imposing our own ideas on the world that we haven't time to receive guidance and inspiration in return. The "daily solo" is the practice of listening.

Silence is one of our most important teachers, for only when we are silent can we begin to hear the voice that is truly directing us—what the Quakers call "the still small voice within."

The process of daily reflection creates perspective and rekindles our energy. When we lose touch with what's primary in our lives, we lose our life energy. We gain back our energy and focus by letting our core values once again guide our daily actions.

At times we are receptive to reflection; at other times we are not. At times triggering events happen in our lives and we are forced to reflect, to go deeper, at other times, we don't sense the need at all.

It's helpful to set aside a definite time—at least fifteen minutes—for a "daily solo" or alone time. It helps to start each day with a solo period, but twilight and evening, before retiring, are also good times.

Try this fifteen-minute solo exercise:

Step 1: Find a place to be alone and sit still.
Step 2: Relax (see next page).
Step 3: Listen.
Step 4: Write in a journal; write about real feelings and priorities. Picture a value or principle you'd like to live this day, or some behavior you'd like to improve. Jot down what you'd need to do. What holds you back or is in the way?

Without a self-training program, you will never understand your internal states and know yourself at all levels. Try this "daily solo" practice for one week, and then judge for yourself its usefulness to you.

Relaxation

A second choice for reducing environmental tension is to change the mind that is dwelling on the situation. The ability to relax totally promotes mental alertness and allows you to act spontaneously and efficiently whenever "triggering events" require you to act. When you were small, the process of relaxing was easy. Since that time, you have been accumulating residual tensions, and you may be convinced that it's difficult for you to relax. It is very simple to relearn the process of relaxation. Think of it as getting back on your old bike. You may wobble a little at first, but you still remember how to use the pedals.

Tenseness occurs in different areas of our bodies. You might carry a large amount of tension in your neck, for example, whereas another person might carry tension in the stomach. Mental tension over "triggering events" is always manifested as physical tension in various parts of your body.

Your muscles are controlled by your mind. You can cause your muscles to completely relax. As you relax, you will find that it is easier for you to concentrate your attention in the direction you choose and to develop a much clearer perception of the events in your life. Try this ten-minute relaxation exercise.

Relaxation Exercise

1. Sit in a comfortable position. Consciously examine your physical tension and describe it to yourself in detail. Examine its intensity. Become as aware as you possibly can of the tension and related discomfort. Tense by tightening up the area; then relax it. If you touch the tense area with your hand, you will feel the discomfort. Interesting areas to try are your jaw, back, neck, and eye muscles. Most people are tense in these areas without being fully aware of it.

2. Close your eyes. Take several slow, deep breaths, breathing from your abdomen. Breathe in and out through your nose, taking breaths that are long and slow. Count "one" as you inhale and "two" as you exhale. Count your breaths over again with each breath cycle for five

minutes. Concentrate on the numbers one and two, saying them to yourself with each breath cycle. The idea here is to clear your mind. Most of us feel controlled by the thoughts that constantly enter our minds. If you consider thoughts as they go through your mind, you realize you have stopped counting and started thinking. Visualize your thoughts as clouds floating toward you, floating freely into your mind, and then floating out of your mind again. Keep going back to counting your breaths. It will become easier as you practice.

3. Describe the effects this breathing has on your body. Do you feel less tense? Over a long period of time, you will definitely feel the effects of relaxation. (See the bibliography for further reading suggestions.)

Creating Your Environment

A third choice is creating an environment that expresses your vision of what you would like your lifestyle to be. This helps get you in harmony with your life and relieves tension. When you are at home or in a community or geographic situation that makes you ill at ease, tensions are created.

Living in life spaces you consciously choose maximizes harmony with your inner self, diminishing tensions and creating more energy. What is your "vision" of the way things should be with your life spaces? Complete the following sequence.

My Life Space

1. Find a place that will be quiet and free of distractions for thirty minutes. Place a pencil and paper next to you. Find a comfortable position.

2. Complete the following sequence. As you do this, keep in mind that some people will picture their "life space," others will get a general feel for it, and still others will systematically list the elements of it. Any approach is fine.

Home space: Imagine yourself in a living space (house, apartment, townhouse) where you feel perfectly at ease and happy. Imagine what the house is made of. Picture the furniture. Sit in a comfortable chair. What is it made of? How does it feel to your touch? Imagine the furnishings and decorations. What style do you picture? What colors surround you? Imagine little things around you—plants, rugs, artifacts, etc.

Geographic space: Get up, walk to the back door, open it, and go outside. What is the landscape like around you? Water? Hills? Plains? Mountains? Trees? What is the climate like? Are there gardens, flowers, fields, forests? Walk two or three blocks away from your dwelling. Imagine the general landscape. Is there a neighborhood? Rural? Urban? Suburban? Foreign? How large is the community? Is it a high-key (major city) or a low-key (small town) community? Imagine the people in the community. What do they look like? What are they doing? Or are you alone? How do you feel right now? Relaxed? Tense? Highlight the life spaces you envisioned in your mind:

3. In the space provided write the ten most important things you considered in your life-space vision (house style, weather, country, university access, etc.).

I "must" have:

1. WARM weather
2. city within 30 min
3. OPEN space
4. WATER
5. _____
6. _____
7. _____
8. _____
9. _____
10. _____

I "want" to have:

1. Mountains
2. _____
3. _____
4. _____
5. _____
6. _____
7. _____
8. _____
9. _____
10. _____

In your ideal life space, which general area of the country or world did you envision yourself in? Small town, farm country, Hills/Mountains, WATER, Rural

Within the general location you selected above, select three places, cities, towns, or suburbs that might fit the specifications you designated in your list.

1. _____
2. _____
3. _____

How do your current life spaces compare with the information above?

4. You can start taking steps toward your ideal life spaces immediately. The effect can be gradual and cumulative (one small change per week, like changing wall colors). That's more than fifty-two changes per year! Or perhaps your life spaces require moving, building a house, changing geographic locations. Consider these immediate options:

   a) Visit a nearby town, city, or neighborhood that most nearly re"sembles your ideal life space. Take pictures of life space areas similar to your goal. Visit with local people.

   b) Subscribe to the newspaper in the area that epitomizes your ideal life space. Get a feel for the lifestyle tone—the issues, opportunities, and businesses that seem most important.

   c) Visit your local library to obtain books that give further ideas about your ideal life space. Is there a publication that tends toward your interest? Ask your librarian.

   d) Take a vacation in an area that resembles your ideal life space. Write the questions you want answered and the people you want to see. Write the Chamber of Commerce for suggestions.

The main point is to provide life spaces where you can relax and be free of tensions imposed by an environment you do not like.

 Enter your preferred life space locations from Question 3 in Box 7 of your Excursion Map.

9   Mind

The mind is a wonderful thing. In our sailing example, the mind is the sailor, the one in control of the boat. In our culture a great deal of time is spent training, educating, and improving our minds. Almost everything we do, including activities we call mindless, requires our mental attention at some level. Our days are made up of communicating, thinking, learning; perhaps organizing, writing, problem solving, creating. We do remarkably well, given the fact we use only 5 percent of our brain's capacity.

Most of us spend the bulk of our time using our left brains, our analytical, verbal side. Exciting research in the past dozen years has opened a new area of investigation, the right brain. That is where visual perception, intuition, invention, and creativity are fostered. Inventurers learn to use not one or the other, but both, to work together in search of peace of mind.

In this chapter we focus on the right-brain/left-brain dichotomy, to jar you into exploration of your own right brain. Then we aply these concepts to the way in which you learn—your learning style. Understanding more fully your mental capacity will give you more choices and more confidence in the career/life renewal process.

THE RIGHT AND LEFT BRAINS

Betty Edwards has written a wonderful book called *Drawing on the Right Side of the Brain*. In it she summarizes the right- and left-brain functions and challenges us to shut off our left brain for a few minutes. We borrow from Betty's writings to share both sides of the brain with you.

Most of us are afraid to draw anything. We think back to our first representations of houses, the sun, flowers, and children with amusement, but when asked to draw the same scenes now, we shriek, "All I can draw are stick figures." We've become stuck, largely because of messages from our left brain, as we shall see in a minute (see figure 9.1).

Now you're asking, "But what does drawing have to do with the two sides of the brain?" To oversimplify the explanation, the two brain halves, right and left, serve quite different functions. According to our current understanding, we need both the left-brain mode of consciousness and the right-brain mode of consciousness. We use both, but many of us are less accustomed to using the right-brain mode, the intuitive one. It is helpful to tap the right brain in order to draw likenesses and to make connections that take us beyond stick figures. Learning to draw is also a good way for those of us left-brain–oriented people to expe-

Figure 9.1.

Child's drawing

rience what the right brain can do. After learning to draw, we can translate the experience to everyday problems as well. In fact, most of this book is an attempt to get you to do life and career planning with both sides of your brain. Keep that in mind as you complete the book. Before we experiment with drawing (relax, it'll be fun), these are the descriptions of the two modes of consciousness.

 MODE

 MODE

Verbal: Using words to name, describe, define.

Nonverbal: Awareness of things, but minimal connection with words.

Analytic: Figuring things out step by step and part by part.

Synthetic: Putting things together to form wholes.

Symbolic: Using a symbol to *stand for* something. For example, the drawn form 👁 stands for *eye*, the sign + stands for the process of addition.

Concrete: Relating to things as they are, at the present moment.

Abstract: Taking out a small bit of information and using it to represent the whole thing.

Analogic: Seeing likenesses between things; understanding metaphoric relationships.

Temporal: Keeping track of time, sequencing one thing after another. Doing first things first, second things second, etc.

Nontemporal: Without a sense of time.

Rational: Drawing conclusions based on *reason* and *facts*.

Nonrational: Not requiring a basis of reason or facts; willingness to suspend judgment.

Digital: Using members as in counting.

Spatial: Seeing where things are in relation to other things, and how parts go together to form a whole.

Logical: Drawing conclusions based on logic: one thing following another in logical order—for example, a mathematical theorem or a well-stated argument.

Intuitive: Making leaps of insight, often based on incomplete patterns, hunches, feelings, or visual images.

Linear: Thinking in terms of linked ideas, one thought directly following another, often leading to a convergent conclusion.

Holistic: Seeing whole things all at once; perceiving the overall patterns and structures, often leading to divergent conclusions.

Figure 9.2. *A comparison of left-brain and right-brain characteristics**

* From *DRAWING ON THE RIGHT SIDE OF THE BRAIN* by Betty Edwards. Copyright © 1979 by Betty Edwards. Reprinted by permission of J. P. Tarcher, Inc.

One of the most graphic examples of the differences between the right and the left brains in drawing is demonstrated in Edwards's book by the Picasso drawing exercise. You are simply to look at one of Picasso's famous drawings (of Igor Stravinsky) and draw it as you see it, only looking at it upside down. The reason for this is that when we look at things right side up we name and categorize them and block our right brains. We don't see shapes but rather "legs," "arms," etc. When we turn the thing upside down, we see shadows, different shapes, new relationships, and angles. If you are wondering about this, just write your signature below, turn the book upside down, and see how different it looks to you.

Signature: _____

Take a deep breath and try this exercise in drawing, even if stick figures were your last attempt. Look at the upside-down Picasso drawing on the next page and draw it upside down according to the directions.

Just to show you that we're good sports, and that we too discovered something, Janet's Picasso rendition is shown as well.

LEARNING STYLES

One of the most insightful and useful tools for adults is the knowledge of their own personal style of learning and changing. The unique way in which you go about gathering information, sorting it out, and making decisions is called your learning style. You are more likely to succeed on your excursions if you are aware of your most enjoyable learning style.

An analogy to illustrate learning styles is that of a futuristic computer, one into which you can put in sounds, shapes, tastes, colors, textures, smells, feelings, movements, and letters. Once the information is inside, the computer, our mind, uses our learning abilities to mix it all together, make sense of it, transpose it, and send it back out of us in the form

Before you begin: Read all of the following instructions.

1. Find a quiet place to draw where no one will interrupt you. Play music if you like. As you shift into R-mode, you may find that the music fades out. Finish the drawing in one sitting, allowing yourself about thirty to forty minutes—move if possible. Set an alarm clock or a timer, if you wish, so that you can forget about keeping time (an L-mode function). And more importantly: *do not turn the drawing right side up until you have finished.* Turning the drawing would cause a shift back to L-mode, which we want to avoid while you are learning to experience the R-mode.

2. Look at the upside-down drawing (Figure 9.3) for a minute. Regard the angles and shapes and lines. You can see that the lines all *fit* together. Where one line ends another starts. The lines lie at certain angles in relation to each other and in relation to the edges of the paper. Curved lines fit into certain spaces. The lines, in fact, form the edges of space, and you can look at the shapes of the spaces within the lines.

3. When you start your drawing, begin at the top and copy each line, moving from line to adjacent line, putting it all together just like a jigsaw puzzle. Don't concern yourself with naming the parts; it's not necessary. In fact, if you come to parts that perhaps you *could name*, such as the H-A-N-D-S or the F-A-C-E (remember, we are not *naming things!*), just continue to think to yourself, "Well, this line curves that way; this line crosses over, making that little shape there; this line is at that angle, compared to the edge of the paper," and so on. Again, try not to think about what the forms are and avoid any attempt to recognize or name the various parts.

4. Begin your upside-down drawings now, working your way through the drawing by moving from line to line, part to adjacent part.

5. Once you've started drawing, you'll find yourself becoming very interested in how the lines go together. By the time you are well into the drawing, your L-mode will have turned off (this is not the kind of task the left hemisphere readily takes to: it's too slow and it's too hard to recognize anything), and your R-mode will have turned on.

Remember that everything you need to know in order to draw the image is *right in front of your eyes*. All of the information is right there, making it easy for you. Don't make it complicated. It really is as simple as that.

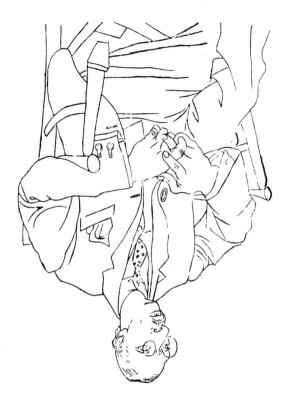

Figure 9.3. Picasso's drawing

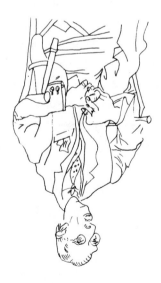

Janet's Picasso

of ideas, speech, words, symbols, facial expressions, and body movements that fit together to form a whole. (See figure 9.4.)

All the information that goes into our own unique and personal computer is processed in some miraculous way, using four major abilities that we all possess. Each of us uses these four abilities in various ways and to different degrees. These four abilities form the basis for our learning styles. They are the following:

1. *Feeling*. Some of us choose and digest learning information primarily because it feels good (we "just know" it when we feel it). We use our emotions or feelings to guide us in deciding what to do in situations and how to proceed. We may use more body movement and speech to learn and communicate. We like having real experiences to get involved in.

2. *Observing*. Others of us use our imagination to observe and digest new material or ideas, seeing them in new ways or drawing mind pictures. We would rather think through ideas using visuals and analogies or write about ideas than verbalize off the tops of our heads. We react to the ideas of others.

3. *Thinking*. Still others of us primarily scrutinize or analyze information, pulling it apart and putting it back together logically. We design models and symbols, taking as much information into account as possible.

4. *Doing*. Some of us see information primarily as part of action, to help solve a problem. We use words and acts to promote a project or a solution. We like to learn while it's happening. We make things happen.

One of the problems with most life and career or other personal-growth programs is that they are taught on the basis of only one major style. Some inventurers like charts and graphs. But for others, charts are like sudden death. Some like the support of a group; others need lots of time alone with the material. *The Inventurers* is written to take all styles into account and to encourage you to identify and then adopt exercises that suit your own style.

Figure 9.4. *The learning "computer"*

People with different learning styles will go about the process of change and growth, or inventuring, in different ways. At points along your life excursion, you will use all of the styles in some way, but as you will find out, you are probably more interested in or more inclined toward one style.

In a minute, you will create a simple, subjective learning-style profile by taking a simple test that we adapted and designed on the basis of the fine work of David Kolb at Case Western University. It will help you understand your learning style better. First, a few introductory words to acquaint you with our intent:

1. Learning profiles and personality tests are only guides that help you capitalize on information that you probably already know at least subconsciously about yourself. No learning style is better than any other; they are just different.
2. No one likes to be categorized and forever stuck in a box. Find out your favorite style, then read about the others and use them along the way too, if you choose.
3. Subjective (self-report) tests depend partially on your mood or state of mind when you take the test and may vary slightly if taken at another time. Use your test results as an indicator. Other people may see you differently, depending on how well they know you. They only know what you choose to show or tell them. But ask others' opinions of you according to the learning-style descriptions and see how closely they agree with your own.
4. Your learning style may vary slightly from situation to situation, or for specific learning tasks, or you may have gained broader learning experiences with age, so that you prefer more than one style. Most of us use basically one most preferred style, but you can shift around and become more flexible in your learning.

Learning Style Inventory

As you complete this inventory, think of the ways you most frequently go about learning. If you are trying something new, how do you learn best? If you are preparing to teach other people about a topic, how do you most easily prepare yourself? Mark A if you strongly identify with the word on the left, B if less so, C if you identify more with the word on the right, D if you strongly identify with the word on the right-hand side. You can begin by completing the sentences that precede each section.

Generally, I learn best by:

	A	B	C	D	
Talking			✓		Listening
Acting		✓			Reacting
Taking small steps				✓	Observing overall picture
Being quick		✓			Being deliberate
Experimenting		✓			Digesting
Carrying out ideas		✓			Thinking up ideas
Changing	✓				Remaining constant
Being animated		✓			Being reserved
Doing	✓				Watching
Being goal-oriented		✓			Being process-oriented
Being practical		✓			Seeing ideals
Changing as I go				✓	Mapping out in advance
Finding solutions			✓		Identifying problems
Formulating answers			✓		Formulating questions

Total the number of As, Bs, Cs, and Ds you checked and write them below.   2   7   3   2

In learning situations, I am:

	1	2	3	4	
Intuitive			✓		Logical
Personally involved	✓				Impersonally objective
Emotional				✓	Intellectual
Supportive		✓			Critical
Eager to discuss with others		✓			Prone to analyze by myself
Interested in new experiences	✓				Interested in new ideas, models
A believer in opinion			✓		A believer in theory
Accepting			✓		Questioning
Feeling			✓		Thinking
A quick risk taker			✓		A slow risk taker
Prone to trial and error			✓		Prone to planning and organizing
People-oriented		✓			Task-oriented
Ready to jump in	✓				Wanting facts first
Dependent				✓	Independent

Total the number of 1s, 2s, 3s, and 4s (if you checked four 2s, you have a total of 4, not 8!). Write them below.

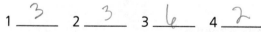

1 _3_ 2 _3_ 3 _6_ 4 _2_

   You've been asked to react to several dimensions of learning. As we sort them out, we find that people identify with some more than with others and that there are four major learning styles. By putting the dimensions together we can explain what each of the learning styles means. (See figure 9.5.)

   In learning new information we rely on a mixture of the four learning abilities we described earlier. Some people rely more on their feelings; others on their thoughts. Some people are very active; others are more laid-back. Your scores will tell you which blend of these factors you favor most.

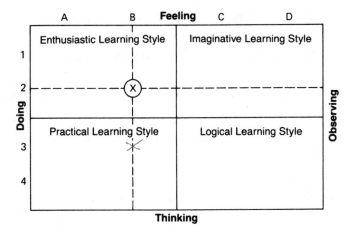

Figure 9.5. *Sample learning style profile*

1. *Imaginative learners.* People who are intuitive-type learners, but who also are deliberate and studied, liking to observe before they act.
2. *Logical learners.* People who are deliberate, unhurried, and also logical thinkers, relating most to ideas.
3. *Practical learners.* People who are thinkers but combine thinking with active problem solving.
4. *Enthusiastic learners.* People who are active, involved, doers who use their feelings as guidelines.

First, look back at your learning-style inventory and find out what your total scores are. Add up the total number of As, Bs, Cs, and Ds, and 1s, 2s, 3s, and 4s. Write them below following the example we've given. Circle your highest score on each line.

A __3__ B __(8)__ C __3__ D __0__
1 __2__ 2 __(7)__ 3 __4__ 4 __1__

A _____ B _____ C _____ D _____
1 _____ 2 _____ 3 _____ 4 _____

Now you need to transfer these scores to the profile in figure 9.6. You do that in three steps.

Step 1. Draw a dotted line down through the boxes, starting from your highest letter score (A, B, C, D).

Step 2. Draw a dotted line across the boxes, starting from your highest number score (1, 2, 3, 4).

Step 3. Mark with a star (★) the place where they intersect. (See example in figure 9.5). That is your most enjoyed learning style. The explanation of each style is in figure 9.7.

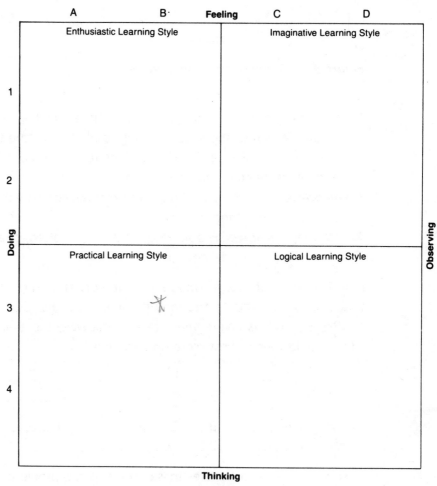

Figure 9.6. *Your learning style profile*

Feeling

Enthusiastic Learning Style	Imaginative Learning Style
Gets involved with lots of new activities —good starter	*Sees lots of alternatives—the whole picture—"Gestalt"*
Operates on trial and error, "gut" reaction	*Uses imagination*
Gets others' opinions, feelings, information, depends on them	*Creates with emotions, aesthetic interest*
Involves and inspires other people	*Oriented to relationships with people, supportive*
Searches, seeks out new experiences	*Uses eyes, ears; listens, observes, asks questions*
Likes risks, excitement, change, incentives	*Observes others, can model behavior*
Dislikes routine	*Good at seeing, imagining self in different situation*
Adapts to situations well	*Unhurried, casual, calm, friendly, avoids conflict*
Willing to try, jump in	*Timing important, can't push until ready*
Can be impulsive	*Likes assurance from others*
Likes learning with people through projects, discussion, "doing"	*Learns by listening, then sharing ideas with small number of people or by modeling*
Practical Learning Style	**Logical Learning Style**
Applies ideas to solving problems	*A good theory builder, planner*
Makes theories useful	*Puts ideas together to form a new model*
Has detective skills; searches and solves	*Good synthesizer*
Tests hypotheses objectively	*Precise, thorough, careful*
Unemotional	*Organized, follows a plan*
Uses reason, logic to meet goals, takes action	*Redesigns, retests, digests*
Speculates on alternatives	*Calculates the probabilities*
Likes to be in control of situation	*Reacts slowly and wants facts*
Sets up projects, pilots with research	*Works independently, thinking, reading*
Acts independently, then gets feedback	*Avoids overinvolvement*
Uses factual data, books, theories	*Pushes mind, analyzes ideas, critiques*
Responsible, takes action on tasks	*Rational, logical, complete*
Learns by working at probabilities and testing them out, coming to conclusions	*Learns by individually thinking through ideas and designing a plan or model in an organized way*

Doing (left axis)   *Observing* (right axis)

Thinking

Figure 9.7. *Learning styles explanation*

If you have ties, it just means that you see yourself as using two styles. If the tie is between B and D, you are probably C. If you score in the corner of any quadrant (A_1, D_1, D_4, A_4), it means that you identify very strongly with that style.

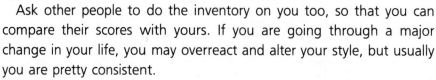 Ask other people to do the inventory on you too, so that you can compare their scores with yours. If you are going through a major change in your life, you may overreact and alter your style, but usually you are pretty consistent.

Remember, only you can decide whether or not you will make changes. This book gives you the tools to use *when* you decide to do it! One of the most important tools is your learning style. Flexibility, or the ability to use many styles of learning, depending on the situation, is a goal to strive for. The more you can shift when you need to, the more satisfied you might be with your overall learning. But remember, you still have a preferred style that you will identify with primarily. *Now you know your preferred style, and you can use it throughout the excursion process.*

To assist you in the experience of life and career renewal, we will explain briefly how each learning-style type approaches the process. Knowing your most preferred style could make the process more enjoyable and productive.

Enthusiastic Learners

They would enjoy "doing" this process with others, talking about the exercises, and trying out several options at once. The process will excite them to test gut reactions and schemes.

Imaginative Learners

Imaginatives like to do the exercises and then let them soak in for a while before acting on them. They will watch what others do and imagine themselves doing the same to see how it feels.

Logical Learners

A thorough, planned approach to the process is most comfortable for logicals. After doing all the exercises and some from other books too, they will wonder how to take action on it all.

Practical Learners

Practicals will scan the book for the exercises that seem most relevant for now. They will finish what they wanted and develop likely options with a plan of attack, before asking how this will affect myself and others.

Learning Styles and Animal Eating Patterns

A fun way to think about different learning styles is to relate them to the way in which various animals eat. This allows us to see all four of the learning styles in a different way, and it also allows us to laugh at ourselves a bit more.

Enthusiastic learners are like monkeys. Monkeys always eat together in social groups. There is no such thing for them as eating alone. They share food, make lots of noise, throw banana peels around, and swing from the branches. They have fun while they eat, in fact if is hard to tell whether eating or fun is the major goal. Enthusiastics like to be with people and see eating and learning as a social occasion first. In fact, if they have fun and meet people they like, the learning experience has been successful for them.

Imaginative learners are like hawks. They soar above the trees, getting a bird's-eye view of the whole scene without having to make any commitments yet. As they circle the scene with perhaps one other bird, they see their lunch scurrying around on the forest floor and when they decide to move, they go after what they want. They are unhurried and very very aware in their relaxed looking flight pattern. Imaginatives have much more going on inside than anyone imagines, and they choose their timing and their eating carefully. In learning, they look over and reflect on what they want, then go after it diligently. They appear to be laid-back most of the time, letting most activity go on inside.

Logical learners are like giraffes. Their long necks and tall stature allow them to quietly and methodically strip the leaves from the trunks to the limbs of the trees for lunch. They eat in small groups and move from one clump of trees to another in systematic fashion. They do not make extra work of it but get it done thoroughly. They are especially careful to stay away from the monkeys who are not only noisy but messy in their eating habits! Being way up with their heads in the trees, they even suggest an ivory tower image of the rational, intellectual type.

They learn systematically and logically, not in large groups or in social gatherings. They gather all the facts, which is what they need, and then move on.

Practical learners are like beavers. There is never just one thing going on when beavers eat. They appear to be just having the tree for lunch, but really they are doing double duty. They will use the tree to make a home for the family, or to make dams. They are always thinking of what other things they could be doing. So lunch is a means to a practical end. So it is with practicals. They eat while making business deals or while reading the paper. Sometimes they even forget to eat, they are so busy. Practicals learn to solve problems, so they take in the information they find pertinent. Tasks are key to them so eating is usually a time for learning or doing.

Sometimes you will find yourself using various learning styles, so one day you will be monkeylike and another day hawklike. Therefore you can be a monk-raffe or a beav-hawk. Usually you have a home style or a major style that reflects your most enjoyable learning style as we said before. Which animal are *you* most like?

 What is the learning style that most reflects you? Enter it in Box 8 on your Excursion Map.

10   Spirit

Of the three factors that determine lifestyle, the spirit or emotional element is the most difficult to describe, probably because it is the last one to develop and mature. This area comprises our life meanings, values, purpose, emotional self, identity, feelings, relationships, and spirituality. Certainly we have a sense of these at younger ages, but frequently we are unaware of them until we have experienced more of life's triggering events.

Spirituality is probably one of the most talked-about and least understood issues of our time. We used to believe we could downplay our spiritual side when we pursued life and career renewal issues. Now we see more clearly how central this issue is to the long-term satisfaction we have in our work and our lives. In fact, for some of us, the career renewal issue comes down ultimately not to what job or career to pursue but to letting ourselves be transformed in the personal and spiritual arenas of life. Transformation has two parts. First is finding out about the inner core of who we are. Second is learning how we live out that core in our lives. Of course, our environment has influenced us and our core, especially in our early years. To be transformed is to learn about the events and the people who have deeply influenced our lives, in positive and negative ways. Then we can see how these happenings affect how we connect with and influence our environment now.

The most effective way to be transformed and find our core, we believe, is to connect with a source of power that is higher and wiser than we are. We need someone or some idea to journey with us and support us in the search for self and meaning. We choose to call that higher power a personal god, but others have other images or symbols for their higher power. For many of us, our early religious or church experiences were so negative or degrading that we cannot now reconnect with a worn-out image of God. We can't yet separate our anger at the church or religion from our need for God. So for a time we choose other experiences to name our spirituality. We substitute many other things for God. We hold on to our control. A loving relationship with a higher power ultimately asks us to let go, not to be in charge, not to be so powerful, but to be called to our selfless purpose in life and work.

The word *vocation* is derived from the Latin word *vocāre*—to be called. We are "called" in the spiritual realm to a new honesty, an inner integrity that gives us a clear way of listening to our life's work calling us. We may not even change our work, but frequently we change the way in which we approach our work. We are no longer "driven"; we are "called" and our higher power guides us to the new ways of being.

But we can't do what we are called to do unless we know who we are, what gives us meaning, what we truly value, what our hidden talents are. This we call inventuring—the search for harmony between the inner you and the outer you. Harmony, like balance, occurs when the pieces, notes, ideas, behaviors are in a satisfactory relationship to each other. Harmony in our lives means having our inner life meanings, values, philosophy, life purpose, and spirituality, in sympathy with our careers. We can be who we really are in all areas of our lives, at least once in a while. This is for most of us a life long endeavor, because it means we're becoming whole.

In addition to working on these issues in this book, we would suggest, if you are serious about developing spiritually, that you seek out a well-trained spiritual teacher or counselor. Spend quiet time listening, talking, praying, walking, in order to hear your own heart's desire and to receive guidance, love, and support from your personal god.

In this chapter, we invite you to look at that harmony in your life, take your spiritual temperature, if you will. We'll explore your personal values, look more closely at the idea of meaning, and explore your life purpose. You may never be the same.

LIFE VALUES AND SPIRITUALITY

Look back at the Life Line Exercise using the excursion model (page 39). Think about what matters most in our life, what you prize or value. Is it a good job, people, risk taking, travel, children, security, health? You can tell by the *consistent* way in which these issues are related to your life events. For example, every low had to do with illness, or every good decision had to do with personal growth and freedom.

We invite you to take a first step in temperature taking by exploring the spiritual highs and lows in your life by means of a Spiritual Life Line. Follow the same directions as for the Life Line, plotting the highs and lows of your spiritual life. You needn't limit yourself to religious or church experiences; include anything you consider spiritual, such as nature experiences, healing experiences, periods of major change, or deaths.

Spiritual Life Line

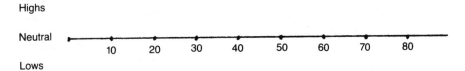

1. What three events have shaped your spiritual life? How?

Baptism

2. What connections do you feel with your childhood religious experiences? *Continue to connect to those religious experiences*

3. How important a factor is spirituality in your life now? *Very important*

Not all of your values will be reflected in your life events. The following exercise gives you a chance to look a little more globally at your values. We are asking you what you believe in or value the most, as exhibited by your present or consistent past behavior.

Life Values Profile

1. Read through the list of life values and rank the values that are reflected by life events or other behavior you consistently show in your life; 1 is high, 20 is low. Don't check what you think you *should* value (for example, "Meaningful work"), but what your behavior *shows*. Use the question "If I were to give up the values one at a time, which would go first, which last?" The last to go is your highest value, 1.

2. Have a special person in your life check the values his/her behavior shows are most important.

My values	Other person's values	
( )	(1)	Achievement (sense of accomplishment/promotion)
( )	(16)	Adventure (exploration, risks, excitement)
( )	(14)	Personal freedom (independence, making own choices)
( )	(19)	Authenticity (being frank and genuinely yourself)

( ) (15) Expertness (being good at something important to you)

( ) (10) Emotional health (ability to handle inner feelings)

( ) (19) Service (contribute to satisfaction of others)

( ) (11) Leadership (having influence and authority)

( ) (20) Money (plenty of money for things you want)

( ) (4) Spirituality (meaning to life, religious belief)

( ) (6) Physical health (attractiveness and vitality)

( ) (9) Meaningful work (relevant and purposeful job)

( ) (5) Affection (warmth, caring, giving and receiving love)

( ) (18) Pleasure (enjoyment, satisfaction, fun)

( ) (12) Wisdom (mature understanding, insight)

( ) (3) Family (happy and contented living situation)

( ) (2) Recognition (being well known, praised for contribution)

( ) (1) Security (having a secure and stable future)

( ) (13) Self-growth (continuing exploration and development)

( ) (8) Mental health (having a keen, active mind)

3. Compare your ranking with that of the special person who filled out the column marked "Other person's values." How are your answers alike? Different?

4. Now write down the top three values that you chose. Which value do you consider 1, 2, 3? What do the three together mean to you?

1. _Security_

2. _Recognition_

3. _Family_

5. Are your values more oriented to mind, body, or spirit? For instance, do you value the physical, intellectual, or emotional realm? Which life factor is most prominent overall? _Emotional_

You will see shortly how values and personal qualities fit into one's life purpose, but first we need to have you address your life issues.

 Enter your top values in Box 9 the Excursion Map.

LIFE MEANING

How long has it been since you asked yourself, "What do I want out of life? Why do I get up in the morning?"

Most of us periodically face a series of fundamental questions:

"Who am I?"
"Why am I here?"
"Why do I get up in the morning?"
"What am I doing with my life—my work?"
"What do I have to contribute that will make a difference?"

In our busy day-to-day lives, our reason for getting up in the morning often becomes blurred. We need to rediscover our life's purpose.

In fact, everyone wants a clear reason to get up in the morning. As humans, we hunger for meaning and purpose in our lives. At the very core of who we are, we need to feel that our lives matter . . . that we do make a difference.

Stop for a moment and reflect on the purpose of your life. At the end of this chapter we will ask you to write it down. Are you satisfied with your answer now? At peace? Many of us secretly feel that there is something missing. A hunger is there, an energy waiting to be tapped; a feeling that our lives are not making a *real* difference. *Purpose* is the name of what is missing.

Purpose, however, is never really missing. Life never lacks purpose.

Purpose is innate—but it is up to each of us individually to discover and express it.

Within the soul of every human being there is a hunger for one's purpose. We all want to know, "What is the purpose of my being here?" "What is my contribution to life?" Ralph Waldo Emerson gave us a clue: "The purpose of life is not to be happy. It is to be useful, to be honorable, to be compassionate, to have it make some difference that you have lived and lived well."

The dictionary defines purpose as "the object toward which one strives or for which something exists; reason for being." It describes purpose*less* as "aimless; pointless."

We believe that everyone has a purpose or a "reason for being." Yet not everyone has detected their purpose. Many of us haven't even thought about our purpose. Others have several purposes. Some people feel they are led to a purpose through spiritual deepening. Others are having a crisis of purpose. Some of us have lost our purpose and are looking for a new one. Many of us fell into ours through someone else or by a crisis or an unexpected event.

The workplace is now a major focus for people to express their purpose in life. Unlike people in former times, many today lack the traditions that tell us what we should do. Now at a loss, it often seems that we no longer know what we really want to do. Since the family, the church, and the community seem no longer to be the cohesive entities they once were, more and more people are expecting work to define "who they are" and to express their sense of purpose. Work is certainly one place to find purpose, but by no means the only place.

The hunger for success so rampant in our society right now mirrors an equally profound bankruptcy of the spirit: an aching need somehow to make a difference—to leave footprints—that can never be achieved by dollars.

Viktor Frankl, a psychologist, author, and professor who is a survivor of Auschwitz, has influenced us a great deal in our search for purpose and meaning. He uses the diagram in figure 10.1 to illustrate his thinking on meaning.

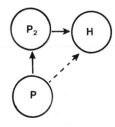

P₂ Purpose
P Person
H Happiness

Figure 10.1.
*Viktor Frankl's
view of meaning*

Pursuing a meaningful goal produces happiness, says Frankl, but if we chase success directly, we are unlikely to get what we seek. There is no enduring happiness in the symbols of success. Our success in seeking out meaning and purpose for our existence determines the happiness we find. Frankl describes three ways in which we ultimately find meaning; (1) in creating a work or doing a deed, which we will call achievements; (2) in experiencing something or encountering some-one, which we will call connectedness; and (3) in our attitude toward unavoidable pain, which we will call suffering. Let's look at what each of these means and ask ourselves about our own meaning.

Achievements: We set goals and we achieve them; we overcome something we thought was impossible; we reach a level of competence, position, or expertise that is very satisfying; we raise healthy children; we finish school; we create something; we do something for someone else. All are examples of finding meaning through achievements.

Connectedness: This area is more amorphous. Frankl means that we experience something like goodness, truth, beauty, justice. We feel we have tapped into a universal mystical experience; or we experience the wonders of nature (sunsets, births, storms) or culture, and we know there is meaning underneath it all; or we encounter another person in their uniqueness by loving them; or we encounter God. All of these experiences bring meaning.

Suffering: Unavoidable suffering is the least inviting base of meaning but perhaps the most profound. It is the attitude and approach we take to life when we are suffering unavoidably—for instance illness, loss of a loved one, abandonment, or torture. We can't change the situation (if it is truly unavoidable), but we change our attitude and make mean-ing from our suffering.

As you think back over your life, from which of these three sources have you derived the most meaning? Cite major examples in the space indicated. Add your own source, if you have a different one.

Past Sources of Meaning

Achievements ___*Work / Sports*___

Connectedness ___*God / Loved ones*___

Suffering ___*Lost Loves*___

Other Sources _____

From which of these sources of meaning do you derive meaning now? Is this a change from the past? Does your Life Values exercise support your idea of your current source of meaning?

PURPOSE IN LIFE

Purpose or meaning is where real success begins. Genuine well-being is a matter of the heart, of a deeply felt commitment, of waking up daily to something larger than our own ambitions.

Of course, the case for purpose has never rested on provable facts or rational logic. Purpose relies on spirit and on the release of human energies generated by hope. The capacity for hope is one of the most significant learnings of life.

We have had the incredible privilege over the last fifteen years of observing many people's hopes. Our observations have led us to some very strong beliefs about hope and purpose, the most important of which we discuss below.

Purpose Is Necessary for Health and Survival

Why do so many people die within about twenty-four months of retiring? Have you known anyone personally who died shortly after retiring?

Having a purpose for living obviously stimulates the will to live. There is a reason to get up in the morning; one's life takes on larger significance.

Many people who have overcome serious illness have been able to identify some important life purpose or goals early in their healing process. After studying the case histories of such people, author Norman

Cousins noted that all of them had experienced some type of crisis just before the diagnosis of their illness. Studies have shown that the most common emotional state preceding the diagnosis of cancer is a sense of hopelessness and despair. To any of us with an appreciation for the relationship between the mind, body, and spirit, this only stands to reason.

There is no agreement on what the purpose of life is, of course, but those who are healthiest in body and soul seem to have defined one for themselves. Not only does a purpose serve as a reason for living, but it becomes a lodestar—the point on which one focuses one's day-to-day energies.

There is much wisdom in the words of Nietzsche: "He who has a why to live for can bear almost any how." What people need for optimum wellness is the striving for some meaningful goal or a purpose that moves them.

Purpose Provides the "True Joy in Life"

If experience alone brought wisdom and joy, then all older adults would be happy, enlightened masters. But wisdom and joy don't come automatically with age. Purpose cannot be ordered into being. It must be discovered. We need to encourage people to rediscover themselves at various ages. They need to be given support for the naturalness of this quest.

With purpose we gain clarity, direction, and relatedness to the greater whole. Purpose provides energy and the feeling of "aliveness"—the primary feeling we're chasing throughout our lives. We want aliveness in our relationships, our bodies, our work, and our spiritual lives.

George Bernard Shaw captured this truth: "This is the true joy in life—the being used for a purpose recognized by yourself as a mighty one; the being thoroughly worn out before you are thrown on the scrap heap; the being a force of Nature instead of a feverish selfish little clod of ailments and grievances complaining that the world will not devote itself to making you happy. . . ."

An inspiring model of "the true joy in life" was the USA for Africa recording "We Are the World," followed by a worldwide simultaneous broadcast of the song by over 5,000 radio stations, followed by the satellite multicity "Live Aid" concert linking some 140 countries.

Bob Geldof, the inspiration behind the broadcasts, said in an interview, "Even if you don't care about the way Africa solves its own problems . . . we cannot every day see these people die on our TV screens. We cannot do it. I cannot do it. And obviously, millions cannot either. But I am not trying to engender a sense of guilt—merely a conceptual leap to understand the world these people live in. As I said in the song, 'Tonight, thank God it's them instead of you.'"

Geldof was asked, "What have you learned in the past year?" His answer: "Having a moral power—and having nothing personally to gain by it—allows you to achieve far more in a given area than were you to do something that had a profit at the end of it."

George Bernard Shaw echoes this feeling: "I am of the opinion that my life belongs to the whole community, and as long as I live, it is my privilege to do for it whatever I can. I want to be thoroughly used up when I die—for the harder I work, the more I live. I rejoice in life for its own sake. Life is no brief candle to me. It is a sort of splendid torch which I've got a hold of for the moment, and I want to make it burn as brightly as possible before handing it on to future generations."

Purpose is finding a good reason for getting up in the morning, ideals worthy of our personal efforts.

Finding Purpose in Your Life and Work

The true story of happiness involves striving toward meaningful goals—goals that awaken us to and enhance a larger purpose.

A good place to start with your purpose exploration is at its roots—with the question "Why do I get up in the morning?"

- "Why do I get up in the morning?" (Repeat the question several times aloud.) Are you comfortable with your answer? Write your answer here. *To go to work.*

- Purpose starts with discovering what is needed and wanted and producing it right where you are! If you had one quarter of your time free to devote to "purpose-full" issues or projects, what would you do? *Working with children or elders*

- We use work to give meaning to our lives, to earn our livelihood, to express our talents and purpose. Is your present work expressing your purpose in life? How? *No*

- How do I find my purpose? One way is to come to grips with your own death. Is it appropriate for you to die? When? Why would it be inappropriate for you to die in five years? If you died tonight, what would you be most disappointed about? (What's left to do or say?) *Spending time family*

- How old do you think you'll live to be? (See page 39, chapter 5)

  ___*92*___   ___*2042*___
  Age   Year

What should you do with the remaining time so that you can look back over your life with few regrets?

Get Closer to family

Your answers to these questions ought to tell you whether or not you have thought about your life purpose, whether you have identified one, and whether you have made a commitment to work on it. Some people have no purpose they can identify.

We are living in a time when the nature and meaning of work are changing radically. It is a time when many people are reconsidering the nature and place of work in their lives. Work is one way of expressing our purpose in life.

A character in John Gardner's *The Art of Living,* Arnold the cook, says it well: "The thing a person's gotta have—a human being—is some kind of center to his life, some one thing he's good at that other people need from him, like, for instance shoemaking. I mean something ordinary but at the same time holy, if you know what I mean." Finding purposeful work is a quest many of us share.

There are times in our lives when we pull back from purposeful activities and times we move into them. This may be dependent on our life stage. The important thing is to think about what you're involved in and why, so it reflects the issues of concern to you. One committed person is worth five who are lukewarm. There never has been a shortage when it comes to good ideas, but the number of people who are moved by an idea, who will risk taking a stand on it, is small indeed.

PROBLEMS THAT NEED SOLVING

Look back over your answers to the questions and decide which problems your purpose helps solve. For instance, if you are involved in cancer research, then health may be your issue, or if you are involved with a battered women's shelter, then the problems of relationships or women's safety may be your issue, or if you are involved in nothing, then. . . .

Here is sampling of issues other people have listed that give them a sense of purpose:

Problems of the poor	Meaningful leisure	Unemployment
Family strength	Women and money	Good government
Increasing	Health	Work ethic
"community"	Spirituality	Youth development
Political change	Minority businesses	Safe neighborhoods
The arts	Education	Prison work or
Protection of	Justice	reform
women's safety	Motivating others	Addiction
Family Play	Housing	World peace
Public TV	Humane	Legal rights
Aging populations	management	Personal growth
Hunger	Child or spouse	
	abuse	

What purpose is the basis for your life?

Having a purpose is one way of being "clear" about questions such as "Why do I get up in the morning?' and about the real bottom line in your life.

 Enter your main life purpose(s) in Box 10 the Excursion Map.

11   Dreams and Goals

Now is your chance to act on the things you've learned in the lifestyle section. It is no small task to summarize lifestyles and life factors or to consider the balance of these factors in your life. Now that you have a broader perspective on your lifestyle, how would you change your three lifestyle factors in size? Maybe working through chapter 10 has confirmed what you thought about your life. Or perhaps you are even more out of balance than you thought. Perhaps at this point in your life you'd like to be *more* out of balance, to expand the size of one of the lifestyle factors!

Here are some examples of ways in which you can expand each of your lifestyle factors—body, mind, and spirit.

Body	**Mind**	**Spirit**
Exercise	Change mindset	Involvement in the arts
Nutrition and diet	Creative pursuits	
Rest	Listening to people, music	Belief system confirmed
Relaxation		
Hobbies using the hands	Getting tasks done	Relationships with others
	Journal writing	
Sports, dance	Work out options	Focus on sensitivity to others, community
Meditation	Self-analysis	
Physical exam	Therapy	Change attitude toward self/others
Improved grooming	Study or school	

Body	Mind	Spirit
Physical image change	Be alone with thoughts	Spirituality
Driving	Games of the mind	Personal awareness
Physical risks	Reading	Humor
Sleep	Imagery and dreams	Awareness of nature
Travel	Research project	Cultivate happy people
Massage	Intellectual hobbies	Take risks
		Music
		Retreats

In the space below, redraw your lifestyle factors (see figure 7.1, page 62) to reflect the percentage of time, interest, and activity *you* want them to take in your life. Compare them with your first lifestyle factors drawing (page 67). What will you do to achieve that balance?

THE POWER OF DREAMS: PUTTING PURPOSE TO WORK

The fantasy is always there. Toss the alarm clock. Say goodbye to routine, to everything ordinary and workaday in your life. Strap on a backpack and head for Europe. Buy a boat and sail off into the sunset. The great dream.

The great dream has much appeal to those of us for whom life can be full of distractions, confusion, and complexity. We all know many people who had the great dream. As children, most of us truly believed we would grow up to travel to exotic places and do unique things with our life's time. In fact, the trial and error of growing up never quite eradicates those dreams.

Although some call it romanticism, it is really a dream that ignites many of us, rekindles our sense of aliveness. In the years we have been working with groups of people struggling to define their dreams for the future, we have encountered few people who did not dream of a "Plan B," with trees, mountains, oceans . . . no clocks or deadlines.

In the rush of modern society, in the attempt to maintain our image as successful persons, many of us feel that we have lost touch with a deeper, more profound part of our beings—our dreams. Yet we feel that we have little time, energy, or support to pursue those areas of life that we know are important.

Like most fifteen-year-old adolescents, John Goddard had a wealth of heart-stopping dreams, starring of course, himself. One ordinary day in 1940 he went to the trouble of writing 127 of his life dreams on a pad of yellow paper. Most lists like that wind up with our report cards in the attic. But his became a blueprint for his life.

In 1972, then forty-seven, he had achieved 103 of his original quests, reported a *Life* magazine article entitled "One Man's Life of No Regrets." By 1986 he had checked off another five of his dreams.

"When I was fifteen," he told the *Life* reporter, "all the adults I knew seemed to complain, 'Oh, if only I'd done this or that when I was younger.' They had let life slip by them. I was sure that if I planned for it, I could have a life of excitement and fun and knowledge."

Why do some people leave the comfort and security of their daily routines to follow their dreams? Volumes have been written on why people take risks.

So, how do you decide whether or not to go ahead, to take the plunge, to act on your dreams to live a life of "no regrets?" Here are five practical steps.

Step 1: Ask Yourself the Tough Questions

First, confront your life on New Year's Day (or any other day for that matter) and ask yourself:

- How am I spending my time right now? *working, financial security*
- Am I living the life I want to live or am I the victim of my earlier programming? *earlier programming*
- What would my lifestyle be like if I could live the way I wanted by virtue of some miracle of overnight change? *Home / Farm*
- What are the things I want to do, be, have, or the places I want to go during my lifetime? *Build home*
- What would I like to work at that would be enjoyable and provide a living for me at the same time?
- How much income do I really require? What could I let go of to achieve my dreams? *House / Boat / Resturants*
- How much of my consumption adds to the clutter and complexity of my life rather than to my satisfaction? *a lot*

Living a life of "no regrets" requires a very tough kind of honesty with yourself and often it means being direct and honest in relationships of all kinds. It often means unburdening our lives—living more lightly, simply.

Step 2: Start a Dream Journal

Journaling costs next to nothing and a journal feeds your fantasies every time you open it. Fill it with lists. Keep a dream list as John Goddard did. How else are you going to fuel your dreams? On a humorous note, you may even want to have a list of things you *never* want to do in your life. It can be very enlightening—to do it and then to ask yourself why you listed these things.

People are generally in love with lists. It starts when they are children, at least when Santa Claus comes to town. "I'm making my list and checking it twice," goes the song.

When you stop to think about it, we all rely on an array of lists. They are truly useful. They save time. They inspire our fantasies. They get results. Here is an example of a dream journal.

Sample Dream Journal
Personal
- Visit the South Pole
- Run a marathon
- Travel through the Grand Canyon on foot
- Learn to kayak and surf
- Read the entire works of Thoreau & Emerson
- Take a cross-country bike trip (with daughter)
- Climb Mount Kilimanjaro and Mount Kenya
- Learn to fly a plane

Career/Work
- Teach a seminar at a corporate learning center
- Work overseas for at least one year; speak French.
- Take a foundation-sponsored sabbatical
- Take early retirement at fifty-five; create a second career in the adventure-travel field
- Write a book on work ethics
- Learn public speaking; be able to charge for speeches
- Publish an article in a business quarterly

Relationships
- Visit birthplace of grandparents with family
- Spend a summer with family traveling through Australia
- Take a spiritual retreat yearly with spouse
- Visit mentor

Spiritual
- Read the Bible cover to cover
- Volunteer for a mission project in Africa
- Become a church deacon
- Visit Vatican City
- Volunteer one evening a week for Hunger Project

Lifestyle
- Live to see the twenty-first century
- Work six months a year; write the other six months
- Explore the possibility of living in Hawaii; try it!
- Create a "zero debts" budget; live simply with little clutter—"plain living and high thinking!"

Step 3: Get Focused—Pick One Goal

A goal is a dream with a timetable. Goals need to be clear, concrete, and written down. They need action steps and target dates that provide constant reinforcement and a sense of accomplishment that sustains your motivation.

Often in our seminars people say, "Well, I don't need to write down my goals because I know what they are." The reason they don't write them down is because it entails making a commitment. If they never write them down, if they never make plans and set deadlines, well, they haven't failed at anything.

For some high achievers who've set and met goals all their lives, their next goal might be to let go of setting goals!

Writing translates vague, semiconscious dreams into commitments. You have more invested in it than before it was written.

Step 4: Picture Your Goal

The skill of visualization (mentally seeing something in vivid detail) is a means of bridging the gap between "what is" and "what can be." The clearer the picture, the easier it is to move forward toward the goal. Undoubtedly some people will find it easier than others, but it can be done by everyone.

Step 5: Budget Your Goal

You need to take a hard look at the cost of the style to which you'd like to become accustomed. A dream does not need to be fueled by a fortune, but it requires, obviously, enough money to survive.

A dream budget is a personal thing, often dependent on what you're willing to give up. A good starting point is to create a "barebones budget" detailing what it will take at a minimum to carry out your dream. What will just the first step cost? Next, open a separate savings or checking account. Building up a cache of any kind has psychological benefits as well as financial ones. If possible, put in a regular small sum. Every time you open that account book, like the journal, it will feed your fantasies and you'll know you're doing something more than dreaming.

In all walks of life, the most alive and satisfied people are the risk takers. They risk believing in their own ideas, taking a stand on their own visions—inventuring.

What do you need to do now in your life so that you will feel you've lived a life of "no regrets" when you reach the end? Norman Cousins wrote in *Anatomy of an Illness,* "The tragedy of life is not death, rather, it is what we allow to die within us while we live."

Life Dream Exercise

It's crucial that you consider what you'd *like* to do with your life in the future—that is, if you want more satisfaction and balance. We're going to assist you by giving you a chance to dream. Pick up your pen and in the next ten minutes (time yourself), write in the space below all the things you want to achieve in the following areas before you die. *Be specific*, for example, "Live in the mountains," "Run six miles a day," "Stay home with the children full time," "Lose weight." Now, get ready, get set, *go*.

Personal—health, fitness, travel, hobbies, schooling, personal growth, travel, adventures: _Finish Degree — Lose weight —_
Continue judo

_____

_____

Career/work—career changes, new positions, second careers, earnings, special projects, new skills, credentials: _____

_____

_____

_____

Relationships—family activities, marriage enrichment, friendships, mentors: _____

_____

_____

_____

Spiritual—spiritual growth, community service, church activities, problems you're interested in solving, people you're interested in helping:
Children /elders

_____

_____

_____

Lifestyle—type of living situations, geographical locale, complexity or simplicity of living, time allocation, life balance:
Log Cabin — Ky

_____

_____

_____

_____

Other _____

_____

_____

_____

Stop!

1. Now pick the *top three* short-term goals you selected and mark them with an asterisk.
2. Next, give each of the three a priority. Which is the most important, second, and third? You must make the choice; that's part of the process.

 Write your Number 1 dream or goal here, and enter it in Box 11 of your Excursion Map.

One way of clarifying how valued a goal is for you is to ask yourself:

1. Am I ready to make a written commitment to that goal?
2. Am I setting a deadline?
3. Is it based on my values?
4. Can I visualize it in considerable detail?

Remember, you can eat an elephant only one bite at a time. Achieving long-term goals is difficult unless you start with the smallest step. But you must start on the first step, or you'll wake up at the age of seventy with nothing but regrets and excuses. We invite you to write your life dream/goal on the Excursion Contract that follows and fill in the information, sharing it with someone who can support your achievement.

Excursion Contract 2

We learn more completely and make deeper commitments when we share with someone else. Your goal is to share with someone what you learned from reading this chapter—within a week.

Share your dreams and Number 1 goal with a mentor or intimate. You'll benefit and so will the person who listens to you. When you share with someone you will clarify your point of view and they will be more likely to support you as you put forth efforts to grow or change.

1. With whom will you share your dream and goal after finishing this chapter?

   _____   _____
   Name   Phone

2. When?

   _____   _____   _____
   Date   Time   Place

3. What are the key insights you'll share? _____

   _____

   _____

   _____

Work Styles

12 Making a Living Work

Work—and the perception of work—are going through some redefinitions. For all our age-old preoccupation with work, we have not as yet been able to come up with a very satisfactory definition of it. Kahlil Gibran defined work as "love made visible." People work for a wide variety of reasons and get various rewards from their efforts. Work is a paradox. We work when we are hungry, and it is obvious that we also work when we are well fed, well clothed, and well housed. We typically devote nearly half of our waking hours to work.

When we devote significant amounts of time to anything, we are implicitly assuming that it is important to do so. Some of us work hard at making a living. Inventurers are seeking ways to "make a living work" for them. They are seeking "good work" as opposed to a "good job."

What are the growing numbers of people who are seeking "good work" trying to find? Good work and a good job are not the same thing. A good job is ofen defined as clean, high-paying, secure, and prestigious. Good work is different. Good work is often defined as "integrated"—something in which who you are and what you do fit together congruently. More specifically, good work includes a harmonious coordination of experience, interests, skills, and conscience—balance of mind, body, and spirit. Like a patchwork quilt with the separate pieces woven together, good work allows us to blend work activities that fit with our values, goals, skills, and interests, or as George Bernard Shaw stated, "to be able to choose the line of greatest advantage instead of yielding in the path of least resistance. . . ." In our quest for good work, we "choose the line of greatest advantage" because we see work in the total context of our lives and understand that we do our best work in those areas in which we are most interested and which fit our abilities.

Work is a paradox. It helps us live with ourselves in many ways. People often say, "I'd go nuts if I didn't work." On the other hand, work often makes it difficult to live with ourselves. A young service station attendant explained his observations this way:

> If they come into the station in the morning, they can still be friendly and act like they're human. But if the same people stop on their way home, watch out! They either just stare straight ahead through their windshields while I fill the tank, or they seem like they're just looking for ways to take it out on me! That's why I try to work weekends.

According to repeated studies, we do not choose to free ourselves from work even if we have a chance. In our own study of a major corporation, we asked 1500 employees (from managers on down), "If you had enough money to live comfortably for the rest of your life, would you continue to work?" Take a minute to answer that question yourself.

Seventy percent in this survey said they would! However, of that 70 percent, 60 percent indicated that they would try to find "good work"—different from a good job. Of course, they all defined good work differently. But the point is that working, particularly at a meaningful type of work, was something most people would voluntarily seek and choose to do. And their definitions of good work were fascinating! It was almost as if they had never thought what working meant to them, but now that they were presented with the "removal" of it, they were able to express feelings that had been there implicitly all the time.

Nearly all of us derive some sense of usefulness and worth from working. Our egos are often so bound up in our jobs that if we were not working (were laid off or retired), our feelings of insignificance might even lead to emotional and physical problems. An old adage states, "To work is to live, and those who do not work seem to die." This literally becomes the case with some people who die shortly after retirement. We usually choose work over idleness, even if we have enough money to live well without working.

Work has many meanings for us:

1. *Personal identity.* When we work, we have a contributing place in society. We feel that we earn the right to be the partner of other people—we earn our membership in society. The fact that someone will pay us for our work is often an indication that what we do is needed by others, thus, we matter as individuals. In fact, this is so important that in our study outlined above, *40 percent* of the people who would choose to work would choose a line of work in which they could make a significant contribution to others, work that would give their lives meaning and purpose. Work is a major social device for our identification as adults. "Who we are" is directly related to "what we do."

2. *Relationships.* When we work, we have a reason to be with others. Most work activity requires interaction and communication. It's not uncommon for people to indicate that the socializing aspects of their work is what they would miss *most* if they retired or did not work. It is not unusual also to find people who live lonely lives after working hours, particularly those people who do not make friends easily. In fact, people often speak of their organization as a "family."

3. *Money.* Realistically, most people need to provide financially for themselves and to protect themselves against possible emergencies as well as the realities of aging. Work has a fundamental economic meaning as a medium for survival. However, there comes a time when money ceases to be our main work motivator. Money is an important incentive to some, not for fundamental financial needs, but because of its symbolic importance. Its acquisition symbolizes for many people power, achievement, success, recognition, and many other things. Sometimes we justify our work by aspiring to a certain position in life—to "arrive." Often our justification is more truly a matter of trying to be loved, through symbolic recognition or prestige.

THE JOB LIVES MODEL

In order to find meaning in our work, we must understand the difference between loss of underlying meaning that results in a life crisis, and the inevitable cycles of work we can expect to experience periodically in our jobs. We need to be careful to ask ourselves the right questions so we are not making problems bigger and harder than necessary.

If we do not ask the questions or see the cycles in our job lives, it can lead to Inner Kill, the process of dying without knowing it. Inner Kill means being emotionally separated from your work. It means loss of creativity and neglect of self-esteem. It means having a hard time getting up in the morning. It means extreme and utter boredom. We all get Inner Kill at one time or another, and few of us know what to do about it. You need to ask the right questions and chart your own career or job progress over time so as to have more choices, sooner. Let's look briefly at the lives of jobs and see how this disease of Inner Kill develops.

1. *The Learning Phase.* When we start a new job we are excited, ready to learn, motivated to do well. We discover a lot and learn the ropes. We hardly have time to think about the next phase because we're so busy. We have a lot of energy.

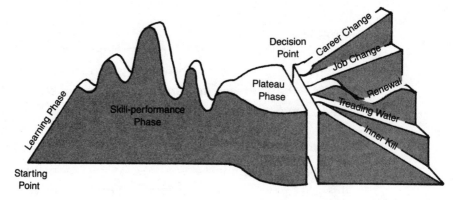

Figure 12.1. *Job lives model*

2. *The Skill/Performance Phase.* This phase allows us to use our skills and to get into the thick of things in our work. We have times of special projects or big events, then a sigh when it is over. Sometimes we get new bosses or we move offices. It is all part of the up-and-down phase of our job. But there always seems to be an up after a down and we continue to feel valued and skilled at what we do.

3. *The Plateau Phase.* No matter how creative or skilled or experienced we are, we will arrive at a point at which we feel less challenged, less energized, less appreciated, less skilled. Or we've been using a skill for so long it's no longer a challenge. Everyone reaches a plateau from time to time, but we feel guilty, as though it's our fault and no one else feels it but us. So we don't talk about it, and usually that prolongs it. In the past, we just waited until a new high came, but now at the plateau everything seems forever flat. It gets harder to be enthusiastic, and easier to be deflated. We are bored, bored, bored. We move along but in no definable direction. Then we come to a decision point, whether we know it or not.

4. *The Decision Point.* At this point we have a variety of options, all of which have different consequences. They are as follows:
   - *Career Change.* Changing into something completely different from what you do now. This is the most difficult and risky of the options. On the average, people now change careers two or three times in a lifetime.
   - *Job Change (in/out).* Changing jobs but staying in the field and in the same general area. Perhaps this would involve moving to another part of the organization, switching jobs with someone else, or moving to a different group. Changing to another organization is more risky but certainly a career option that many people use. We change jobs seven to ten times in a lifetime on the average.
   - *Renewal.* Renewing oneself on the job is a very practical and useful option and could be done before reaching the decision point if you can feel the plateau soon enough. It involves finding new and enriching changes in your work and can be continued indefinitely. More on this later.

- *Treading Water*. This is an option selected by many because it appears to take the least amount of effort. It is not risky on the surface and lets you postpone a decision. It involves doing nothing to reduce the effects of the plateau, not discussing the issues, yet becoming more bored and afraid. Unfortunately, it takes enormous energy after a while just to stay afloat, and sooner or later Inner Kill sets in.
- *Inner Kill*. The last resort or the deepest ailment. It is the time at which you start to erode from the inside, to withdraw emotionally. Chronic crabbiness, extreme behavior, escapism, and self-delusion are all part of it. At this point both your personal life and your job are affected by your unhappiness and self-inflicted pain. You need to act immediately to get yourself out of Inner Kill.

1. Where are you in the job life model now?

2. How long has each of your past job lives been? Your career lives?

3. Is there a pattern? Where is it?

4. How can you predict when you are hitting a plateau?

5. What have you done to get out of or to avoid Inner Kill in the past?

WORK HISTORY

The following exercise is designed to help you review your work history, concentrating on key jobs and their impact on you. Although it provides only a quick perspective on these key experiences, it can be used to discover how your unique pattern of work experiences fits together to direct your current choices. Several exercises in this book will focus on these key jobs or experiences, so think carefully as you review your work life. It can also tell you how you avoided or contracted Inner Kill in previous work experiences.

Work Cycle Exercise

Step 1:   Construct in chronological order on the grid that follows a summary of the work experiences in your life such as full-time jobs, significant jobs and career changes, promotions, demotions, transfers, etc. Include jobs as far back as you feel is appropriate.

Work Cycle Grid

For each major job think back and answer these questions:

- What were your primary responsibilities?
- What were your most enjoyed achievements?
- What type of supervisory style did you work under?
- What were your hours? What was your travel schedule?
- What kinds of people did you work with?
- What kind of product or service you were offering?
- What lessons did you learn?

High Points Average Low Points	
Job or Title (include promotion, transfer, layoff, firing)	
Year	

Step 2: Place dots in the space provided at the top of the grid to represent how high or low each situation was to you. Connect the high and low points by drawing a line between the dots.

Step 3: Pick the two best and two worst work experiences. Answer the following questions about them.

1. Whom did I work for?
   Best: Worst:

2. What did I like most, least about the job?
   Best: Worst:

3. Who did I work with?
   Best: Worst:

4. What were my challenges?
   Best: Worst:

5. What was my environment like?
   Best: Worst:

 Step 4: Summarize in Box 12 of your Excursion Map on pages 188–189 three important work insights you got from this exercise.

WHY DO I WORK?

In recent years studies of work motivation frequently have emphasized a variety of important work meanings. Psychologist Abraham Maslow theorized that needs are the primary influences on our behavior. When a particular need emerges in us, it determines our motivations, priorities, and actions. Motivated behavior is the result of the tension—pleasant or unpleasant—experienced when a need emerges. Our actions reduce this tension. Thus, unsatisfied needs are the primary motivators that get

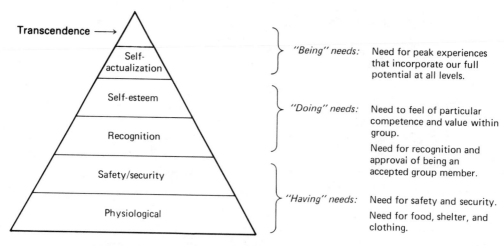

Figure 12.2. *Maslow's hierarchy of needs*

us to act. Maslow defined five levels of needs, which he arranged in ascending order to create a pyramid model (fig. 12.2).

When we satisfy our needs at one level of the pyramid, we move next to satisfy our new needs at the level immediately above that. Like a hiker going up a mountain, we are continually seeking to reach the top of the pyramid. A storm may come along and send us scurrying back down for safety, food, and shelter at the base of the pyramid. But as those needs are met, we again begin the ascent.

On the right side of the pyramid model (figure 12.2), our work-related needs are summarized in three levels:

1. *"Having" needs.* The basic needs for food, shelter, and clothing are met in most "jobs." "Just a job," a phrase often heard, satisfies our basic-level (having) needs of life by providing the money to purchase material goods, food, housing, and clothing. How much of your paycheck do you spend just to maintain your spending patterns? Does money represent a game, a challenge, to you?

2. *"Doing" needs.* The need to accomplish something, do something well, and be recognized for it often comes through success or competence in a chosen vocation. It is more than "just a job." Perhaps

we are working in a particular field, for a special idea, or for a particular organization or leader. As people work their way up an organization or as they get older, these doing needs seem more prevalent. In what kinds of work situations would you work harder than you ordinarily do, putting out more energy and enthusiasm because you felt the work deserved it?

3. *"Being" needs.* These needs arise when we desire more personal fulfillment. We may want to make a more lasting impact. We may feel a sense of mission or cause on an issue we identify with. There is a need to experience a spiritual, intellectual, or aesthetic dimension, a more fulfilling "quality of life." Our spare time or leisure interests often reflect this need. If you could use your work to indulge your favorite interest or form of play, what would you be doing?

Visualizing this, some of us are fortunate enough to have all need areas met through our work situations. Others of us might get one or two needs met. And some of us might experience the higher levels of need satisfaction through aspects of our lives other than work (church, family, hobbies, professional groups). (See figure 12.3.)

Some of us make work out of play, and some of us make play out

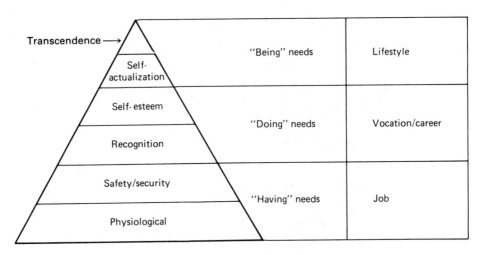

Figure 12.3. *Integration of needs and activities*

of work. Why do you work? What's your definition of "good work"? Being aware of your needs and priorities is an important aspect of your own excursion process. The exercise that follows is designed to help you define "good work" and set work-related priorities.

Why Do I Work?

Consider the following fourteen work-related needs. In column A, rank the items 1 to 14 according to what you want out of work (1 is high; 14 is low). In column B, rank the items (1 to 14) according to what you are getting from your present job. By the end of the exercise, you should be able to say, "I need _____ more than _____, and more than _____." Think of your needs in terms of the work setting rather than overall personal needs.

How have you experienced your work-value preferences in present and previous jobs or work activities? Write at the top of columns C and D titles or key words for work activities or jobs you've had in the past few years. Rank the values *that were present* in each activity or job.

	A Values I want	B Present job I have	C 	D
			Previous jobs I've had	
A. Recognition and approval (self and work known)	_____	_____	_____	_____
B. Variety (having new and different tasks)	_____	_____	_____	_____
C. Socioeconomic status (work meets material needs)	_____	_____	_____	_____
D. Teamwork (work dependent on others)	_____	_____	_____	_____
E. Economic security (continuing income assured)	_____	_____	_____	_____
F. Interpersonal relations (being accepted and belong)	_____	_____	_____	_____

G. Mastery, skill, and achievement (doing a task well
according to one's own
standards)   _____ _____ _____ _____

H. Independence (directing
one's own behavior)   _____ _____ _____ _____

I. Service and social welfare
(having one's efforts result
in benefits to others)   _____ _____ _____ _____

J. Leadership and personal
power (directing and influ-
encing others)   _____ _____ _____ _____

K. Creativity and challenge
(solving new problems, producing new and original
work)   _____ _____ _____ _____

L. Adventure (situations with
risk and change)   _____ _____ _____ _____

M. Self-expression (behavior
consistent with self-
concept)

N. Moral value (behavior con-
sistent with moral code)   _____ _____ _____ _____

Compare your preferences (column A) with your work experiences
(columns B, C, and D). Now answer the following questions:

1. In my present work, I need more _____ ,
_____ , and _____ .

2. My best job match with my present values was _____ .

3. My present job's work values and reward structures show that what
I do is worth spending part of my life on. _____ No _____ Yes
Comment: _____

_____

_____

4. My future work will require _____ , and _____
_____ .
5. My idea of "good work" is _____ .
6. The way in which I get most meaning from my work is _____ .
7. On the Maslow hierarchy, do my values reflect having, doing, or being needs most strongly? _____.

 Enter your top three work-value preferences in Box 13 on the Excursion map.

WHAT'S THE POINT OF WORKING?

The big question when we were children was "What do you want to be when you grow up?" It was too early, perhaps, to ask, "What sort of life do you want to be living when you grow up?"

The modern dilemma, as sociologist Max Weber put it, is "Do we work to live or live to work?"

As we observe the lives of people who have chosen to inventure, two clear themes emerge: integration and balance. The hunger for a balanced life is expressed in one way or another in workshop after workshop, as is a desire to erase hard lines separating learning, work, and retirement.

Many people are inventing new lifestyles, forging new views of good work, and new definitions of success. Success has different meanings at different ages and stages of life.

Pursuit of happiness does not necessarily produce health and well-being. We are a society of notoriously unhappy people—lonely, bored, dependent people who often are happy only when they have killed the time we are trying so hard to save. Many people are discovering that it doesn't make much sense to sell your soul for security and have no time left to do the things—or be with the people—you love.

Many people endure their work because they see no other way to make a living. In addition, their work organizes, routinizes, and structures their lives. At the very least, most jobs force us into a rhythm of weekend leisure, Monday blues, Friday's T.G.I.F., and regular paychecks. Our minds and bodies become so attuned to these rhythms that we barely notice them.

As we shift from an industrial to an information economy, the reasons for which people work—survival and purpose—continue to evolve.

Initially, way back when, work was a means, never an end in itself. We worked to provide the necessities of life and to create leisure and enjoy life.

Machines were invented to produce the necessities of life more easily. However, to keep the machines humming and the economy expanding, we created new sets of needs. Style and model changes were created. Before we realized what was happening, luxuries became psychological necessities.

Our self-worth gradually became associated with what we possessed and consumed. The status people—defined as "the happy ones"—were those with the most toys. Work became the activity that men and women engaged in to provide the new necessities.

Our loyalties and our identities gradually shifted to work. For newly affluent workers, the answer to the question "What do you do?" could become the ticket to a sense of worth. The job began to govern where we lived, how we measured success, and whom we chose as our friends.

As work has become even more central to our identity, we have forgotten that we originally agreed to labor to obtain leisure and to contemplate and enjoy life.

Michael Phillips observes in *The Briarpatch Book*, "In the past it was considered reasonable for people to develop a marketable skill and pursue a career that would earn them enough money to do the things they really wanted to do. People worked at their jobs so they could do the things they wanted on weekends, go where they wanted on vacations and, in some cases, earn enough to retire 'early' and then do what they wanted. Now our peers are saying, 'That's nonsense; why should I do something I don't like 70 percent of my life so I can do what I want 30 percent?'"

Today, more people are using their work as a context for fulfilling both survival and purpose needs. The work world can offer a way of success and service.

Many people use their jobs to help them sort their lives out, to bring different parts of their lives into alignment. If one idea can sum up the inventure process, it is that life has more meaning if outer success balances with inner success. Succeeding inside yourself means discovering and expressing your core. The quality of our lives and the quality of our work time become one and the same.

As people seek to balance survival and purpose, the really tough question becomes "What do I want?"

To have this balance, you have to begin with the question "When challenged by work pressures, how committed will I be to living my values . . . walking my talk?" Living your priorities starts by asking such questions.

If you believe that inner and outer realms of success are at odds, you may worry that you can develop one only at the expense of the other. But simple material success is hollow unless it feeds our inner hunger—a process that is the exact opposite of the idea of burnout. Although burnout is considered to be the result of overdoing, one of its chief causes is "underbeing," an imbalance of energy between inner and outer activity, survival and purpose.

13   The $corecard

Money. Think about it. Money is the most often discussed yet least understood commodity in our society. Unfortunately, it is the "$corecard" for the game of living—the scorecard for self-esteem in our society. In fact, most social and work gatherings inevitably drift back to discussing money. "How much are they worth?" "What did they pay for that?" Along with the weather, discourse about money has become a national pastime. Money is the "most talked about game in town."

Yet for all our preoccupation with money, we know very little about how and why money affects us. Of course, we all know the standard folklore about money that has endured largely unquestioned since the beginning of the Industrial Revolution:

- "A penny saved is a penny earned."
- "If it's worth doing, it's worth doing well."
- "Waste not, want not."
- "Penny-wise, pound foolish."
- "Idle hands are a devil's workshop."
- "Never put off until tomorrow what you can do today."
- "Work before play."

These quotes reflect the values of thrift and work. Productivity and money are supposed to be the main motives, if not the only ones, of most people for working.

Of course, work has a fundamental economic meaning as a medium for survival. The need for money is a basic, but rarely the only, reason for working. And when people are able to earn enough to meet their fundamental "having" needs, other needs become proportionately more important to them.

Numerous studies have shown that when supervisors are asked to rate the factors that motivate their subordinates, money is nearly always at or near the top of the list. When the people themselves are asked to rate their own motives, however, money is usually ranked below such factors as job security, job interest, and agreeable co-workers. The question "Who is right?" is neither answerable nor important. Both groups are reporting the reality they choose to see. How did you rank money (i.e., socioeconomic status and economic security) in the exercise on pages 136–137.

It seems that many of us intend to enjoy the good life through financial independence, but very few of us ever achieve it. According to insurance industry observations, of every hundred people born in the United States, only *ten* are alive and have an independent income at age sixty-five. What has happened to the other ninety people? Thirty-six are dead before sixty-five, and fifty-four more are broke, eking out their retirement years on social security and maybe a pension, or worse, depending on support from relatives or welfare payments.

On the basis of these statistics, our financial probabilities seem like the odds in a card game. There is an important difference, however. In cards, you at least know the rules of the game when you sit down to play. You also know that you can drop out whenever you please. We can't always drop out of the money game as easily. ("Responsibilities, you know!") We often don't even consider our odds, or define our reasons, for playing the money game—perhaps because we don't dare! If we care to learn about the odds, however, we can play the game better. And if we don't like the odds, *we can change the game*.

We must not discount the importance of money. It is a complex factor influencing many areas. Money takes on different meanings for different people. In addition to being a medium of exchange, its supposed purpose, it becomes a symbol of other values. To some people, money represents social respectability; to others, recognition for achievement; to still others, worldliness, materialism, and the "root of all evil." Since money *can* represent the "scorecard" in our lives, we must at least define the rules in the game we're going to play.

The money game is one of continuous action. Satisfaction from money comes usually from an *increasing* income, not from income itself. We are continuously keeping score! We often feel that our current income is something we have already earned, rather than something to be appreciated. When's the last time, after a salary increase, that you said to yourself, "This is great. I'm really going to put out this year for dear old XYZ organization." We spend more time being dissatisfied with our incomes than being satisfied. Why is this?

One explanation for keeping continuous score is the notion preached by advertising and marketing strategists that we have an insatiable appetite for upgrading our standard of living. We focus our attention on the visible "scorecard" rather than on the invisible reality of our lives. When we're insecure, we seek money to make us feel secure again. We try to make more money, buy clothes, etc., to bolster our sagging self-images. Satisfaction is sought through the tangible "score-card"—money. When we want to make a career or lifestyle change, we use money as a defense against change: "I'd probably have to take a cut in pay." A rationalization for inertia is sought in the tangible defense—money—rather than the intangible—fear of failure.

Few people are indifferent to money. Many people think they need a lot of money to be happy. Others think that having only a little money somehow makes them more virtuous. Neither is true.

Money is important up to a point. What is important to understand is our attitude toward money—what is represents to us. It isn't totally a question of how much money one makes, but of how one makes it, and how one uses it.

Henry David Thoreau captures the point: "The cost of a thing is the amount of what I call life which is required to be exchanged for it, immediately or in the long run. . . . Money is not required to buy one necessity of the soul."

In our society, money is an obvious necessity. Money matters. To the average employed or self-employed person, money and its acquisition are extremely important. Our society is upwardly mobile.

There are hundreds of books about how to turn money into more money (the best way to get rich might be to tell other people how to get rich!). But even with all the attention, most people keep money matters secret.

When we gave career counseling sessions, one of our first questions to our client would be, "How much do you earn?" It was always a bit of a challenge to get people to talk about money. The key question we were trying to help clients answer was "Do you rule money or does money rule you?" Knowing yourself means many different things. It means knowing what is most important in your life. It means ordering your priorities, knowing what you can safely compromise—and knowing which compromises of your values and priorities will be deadly.

You really have to know how important money is in your life. The big question is "What sort of trade-off am I willing to make between my money and my time?" Carefully tracking your checkbook and your calendar can be a very revealing experience. When you really dig into the money issue, you may very well be surprised. The question is how much of your time you want to devote to earning a living, and what you want to do with the rest of your time.

Many people at some point in their lives find themselves running ever harder to compete in a race in which they have secretly lost interest. Boredom and routine carry them along in the workplace; real interests have to be squeezed into the brief hours on the fringes of the working day. Open or hidden stress generated in these common situations has a negative impact on physical and mental well-being.

Michael Phillips and Salli Rasberry have explored the illusions related to money and the way illusion works in our lives. They write of "the four illusions about money."*

1. *A lot of money will let me be free to do what I want to do.* Sounds plausible. Think of all the things you might do if you did not have to

---

* From *The Seven Laws of Money* by Michael Phillips. Copyright © 1974 by Michael Phillips. Reprinted by permission of Random House, Inc.

spend your days working to earn a living. However, this attitude leads to trouble if you postpone what you really want to do in life with the rationalization that you will do it later, after you have made more money or retired.

2. *People with a lot of money command more respect than others.* Esteem will come to you if you live a loving, purposeful life. All the money in the world will not buy your esteem, just as all the money in the world will not buy you love.

3. *I need money for my family.* Many of us who get caught up in this illusion spend so much time making money that we don't have time to spend with our families. "Breadwinner burnout" is the unfortunate result. The breadwinner wakes up one morning feeling that he or she is working all the time and has none of the things worth working for. Rather than feeling good about the family, he or she feels resentful. Those who become most trapped by this illusion are often the most closemouthed about family finances. They take on the family's burdens internally. One helpful solution is to have a full and frank discussion about family finances with the entire family.

4. *Money is necessary for security in old age.* True, money can buy one kind of security. But the best security for old age is you. Too many older people who do not want for money are, nevertheless, dreadfully unhappy. Who you are as a person, not how much money you have, is the most important basis for security in old age. People who are open, growing and loving have the most secure old age because they are surrounded by friends and family who love them and care about them.

Which of the following best describes how you feel about your current financial status?
- ☐ My monthly expenses exceed my income.
- ☐ My income covers the basics with nothing left over.
- ☐ My income meets the basic needs with some money left over.
- ☐ I have money for savings, investments, and enjoyable purchases.

☐ I am becoming financially secure and independent.
☐ I try not to think about money, but about what needs doing.
☐ Other: _____

What is your desired income level five years from now? _____

Does your area or field have the potential to meet your income expectations? ☐Yes   ☐ No   ☐ Not Sure, What changes in your field would you need to make and what risks are you willing to take to earn more money?

_____

_____

Would you ever consider making less money in order to do what you really *want* to do? ☐ Yes   ☐ No   ☐ Not Sure

  Enter a summary of your financial goals in Box 14 the Excursion Map.

Money is a problem for everyone sometimes. We encourage individual ambition and success as the American way of life, yet we often criticize people for having traded their feelings and values for monetary gain. We preach the values of more and less. In his book, *The Money Personality*, Sidney Lecker calls this our "schizophrenic approach to monetary success."

Living well does not necessarily depend on having more money or more things. Needs and expenses, as many may have noticed, have an incredible way of rising to keep up with income!

If, like most of us, you don't have enough money, there are basically two things you can do: 1) increase your income, or 2) simplify your life.
Duane Elgin points out in his book, *Voluntary Simplicity:*

We all know where our lives are unnecessarily complicated. We are all painfully aware of the distractions, clutter and pretense that weigh upon our lives and make our passage through the world more cumbersome and awkward. To live with simplicity is to unburden our lives: consuming, working, learning, relating and so on.

What's alternative today is mainstream tomorrow. Elgin reports that as many as 5 percent of all Americans are consciously exploring a lifestyle of voluntary simplicity—and right livelihood—with more emphasis on self-sufficiency, conservation, cooperation and community.

With the title of his book, *Small Is Beautiful*, the philosopher E. F. Schumacher provided a motto for this shift in values. His philosophy rejects the ideal of exponential growth and the ethic of "More is better." Notice, he says, that "the amount of time people have is in inverse proportion to the amount of labor-saving machinery they employ."

The people Schumacher calls home comers recall what life is really about and trade the lust for more goods and the compulsion to work for more time, silence, and simplicity.

Inventuring inspires a balance between working to live and living to work.

SOUL AND MONEY

Many people engage in life and career planning to strike a new balance between soul and money. Money is their primary obstacle in making changes. They say, "How can I make changes in my life with all these financial responsibilities? It's easy for *you* to make changes; you don't have kids! You have two incomes! You don't have a house! You've saved enough!" And so it goes—the postponed life continues.

How do you make the change? We always give the same advice: "You start doing it in small ways." Money will come when you're doing the right thing. Most people question that statement. Consider a few of the styles of coping that people have used to deal with the money issue, however:

- Figure out on paper exactly how much you are talking about. We operate on myths and fear in the money area.
- Adhere to a strict, barebones budget.
- Start saving now for the future goals you have.
- Share the risk with a partner; start slowly and small.

- Refinance your home or move to a smaller one.
- Creatively moonlight.
- Borrow money.
- Depend on spouse's income or make arrangements with a friend to take turns with expenses.
- Sell all your seldom-used possessions.
- Reduce your lifestyle temporarily; use your vacation money to further your goal.
- Form an inventure society to design new financial alternatives.
- Others: _____

What we must ask is not how much money we need to prosper, but what conditions of life and personal relations are necessary to make us happy. What do you want the quality of your life to be? That's the optimum scorecard. Then what will it take financially to make that happen? We're often surprised at the answer!

14 Skills, the Root of All . . .

Many of us think of ourselves as roles, as titles. And then we determine our personal status and worth by the amount of prestige and recognition those titles suggest. Oftentimes, money is associated with the status, although not always. Imagine yourself at a party, overhearing these introductions:

"Hello, who are you?"

"I'm Hal. I'm with Sally. She just started with the company as a marketing specialist. She is over there with the president of the company. What's your name? And what do you do?"

"Well, Hal, I'm Herb. I'm the treasurer of this operation. And this is my wife, June."

"Hello, June. Do you work too?"

"No, I'm just a housewife."

Despite all our new awarenesses, we still hear people saying these things. So far, we know nothing about Hal except that his spouse talks to the president. June has just put herself down, not because of what she does, but because of the way she portrays herself. Herb started the whole thing and now is at a dead end. Where would you go with the conversation now?

Our job titles seem to speak louder than "who we are." Role or title myths often rule the way we treat one another and ourselves. Several myths are most commonly used: paid work is better than unpaid; "women's work" is degrading; the more powerful the position, the more impressive the person; working with your hands is not as prestigious as working with your head; the status of academic jobs outweighs the financial rewards; service occupations ought to expect low pay; business, though stressful, holds long-term financial rewards; there are many jobs women should never attempt; you can always fall back on sales.

Of course, *all* of these myths are being challenged now, and rightly so, because we are learning that there is more to work than titles, prestige, and money. Besides, job titles tell us little, if anything, about what a person does during the day, what skills are used, and what special qualities that person brings to the job. Think of the differences among these women: a homemaker who has a retarded child to care for, another who is a poetry writer, and another who is president of the League of Women Voters.

In this chapter, you will be introduced to an alternative way to think about your skills in relation to your work and daily activities—a way that will make sense and will stress what you can *do*, what you're *good at*, and what you *like* to do—rather than giving you a title that automatically categorizes you. Other people determine 75 percent of their opinion of you by the way in which *you* present yourself to them. The other 25 percent is determined by your actual work, skills, and reputation. If *you* are not aware and convinced of your skills, qualities, special traits, wants, and interests, you can't expect others to read your mind and know them. Not even your spouse or closest friend can do that.

A woman shared this story recently. "I always thought that getting into management was the way for me to make it and be successful. When I got there and did it for a while I found I kept trying to cover up the fact that I really didn't like managing other people. I had a real crisis in my career when I looked at my skills and discovered I never wanted to manage people again. Now that I am back in research and development work on a small team I've gotten my creativity back. I'm alive again, and happier than I've been before in my whole career."

As a result of working diligently on skills exercises such as the ones in this chapter, one man found a great discrepancy between his job and some of his most enjoyed skills. He was physically and mechanically oriented, and was in a management position. He remembered how much he'd enjoyed working on cars in high school. So now, instead of leaving his job to become an auto mechanic, he started collecting and fixing old cars. He had balance in his life and the frustrations he felt with his work diminished considerably.

THE SKILLS TREE

Skills are a constant part of our everyday vocabulary: "I'd like to go back to work, but I'm not sure I have the right skills." "To shift careers, I'd have to go back and be retrained." "I graduated with four years of college and no skills to get a job." However, few of us can even define the term "skill," much less state what our own skills are.

One of the key parts of the excursion process is to focus on your skills—particularly those you would most enjoy using at this point in your life cycle. Identifying skills is a difficult task for most of us. A simple and concrete tree analogy will illustrate the three important skills areas that you possess (figure 14.1).

1. *The root system*. Each tree must acquire food and water at least partially through its root system. The roots are not visible above the ground, but are necessary to the growth and development of the tree. The roots do most of the work to support the tree and seek out nutrients. So, too, with our root skills. They are not obvious, but are the essential tools we use, our practical performance.
2. *The soil*. The soil is the medium in which the tree grows. The soil must contain nutrients that can be transmitted by the roots to the tree so that the growth of the tree can be maximized. If the soil is depleted of nutrients or lacks moisture, eventually the tree will show the effects. The way in which we adapt to our environment is seen as our survival skill. Do we flourish or die? Do we know what soil/ environment is best for us?

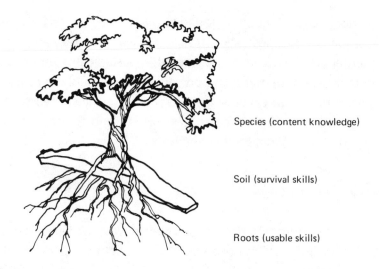

Species (content knowledge)

Soil (survival skills)

Roots (usable skills)

Figure 14.1. *The skills tree*

3. *Species.* There is quite a difference between a palm tree and a flowering crab, an evergreen and an elm or maple. They are all separate species, live in different places, grow in different ways, and have unique phases or cycles. Our species is shown by our knowledge, our expertise on subject matter. These skills are perhaps the most obvious because they can be traced easily to degrees, training, titles.

ROOT SKILLS

Just like the roots of a tree, your root skills (root system) are not obviously visible, but they are your essential tools in performing in the world of work. Your root skills are your portable, transferable, usable skills. They are stated as actual things you can do (skills you have), and they express the action you perform in work situations.

Root skills are the ones you take with you and use, no matter what job you have, no matter where you are. You gain them particularly from experience. So the more varied experiences you've had, the more root skills you'll have. You carry your root skills with you, but may have to use them occasionally to keep in practice. They are not the kind of skills you leave in your desk when you complete a work activity or change jobs. They are portable—they always go with you!

Here are some examples of root skills:

learning	analyzing	filing
managing	singing	organizing
interviewing	designing	translating
lifting	directing	writing
listening	assembling	counseling
modeling	researching	

The intriguing thing about root skills is that we are always shocked at how universal they are. The myth is that different jobs or careers require unique skills that only people in those fields possess. This is usually not the case. Counselors and salespeople, for example, use many of the same root skills (listening, diagnosing, showing empathy). Similarly, both lawyers and computer programmers use many of the same root skills (analyzing, designing, strategizing, implementing plans). What is different for each are the problems and content knowledge of their work, in addition to the language used.

Beyond a certain basic level of training in most fields, the way in which you can best decide what you want to do next is to choose the root skills you most enjoy using and look for jobs and careers that will enhance the use of those skills. Often we let supervisors or random chance totally determine our use of root skills on the job. We hope that our supervisor can read our minds and magically choose the jobs that will make best use of our skills. Inventurers, however, have seen the disappointments that mind reading brings. They are willing to take the risk to share with their supervisors the root skills they have and really enjoy using. Nine times out of ten, supervisors are thankful and very relieved that they finally know enough information to make more constructive plans.

There is no simple test or way to find out what root skills you have, although a number of ways have been attempted. The range includes mechanically scored tests, lengthy autobiographical papers, personal interviews, and previous work-assessment procedures. The best procedure for you will be partially determined by your learning style and by the amount of perseverance you have. So prepare yourself for a skills workout on the Root Skills Checklist that follows.

In addition to our Root Skills Checklist, we also recommend John Crystal's autobiographical method and Dick Bolles's Quick Job Hunting Map as alternatives (see the bibliography). The Job Hunting Map and the Root Skills Checklist are based on John Holland and Sidney Fine's categories of people and environments.

The Root Skills Checklist

We have designed a simple, straightforward method of approaching the checklist. You will complete the checklist several times, following the instructions below, and then compare your scores to see what you find.

Step 1. First, make a copy of the entire checklist for someone else—boss, mentor, or friend—to complete. Give this person the checklist, asking her to check in column 6 the ten to fifteen skills they think you are best at.

Step 2. Scan the checklist in its entirety. Then go back to the beginning and in column 1, "Overall impression," put a check (√) next to the skills that you generally feel you can do (because you have done them before). Now go back over those that you have checked and circle the ten skills you enjoy the most, from the entire checklist, (⊘).

Step 3. Move to column 2, "Present job." Go through the checklist again, checking only those skills you actually use on your present job. Put two checks (√√) by those skills you feel you are best at.

Step 4. In columns 3, 4, and 5 we ask you to go back to three previous jobs or experiences in life in which you felt competent, fulfilled, happy, satisfied, or in which you accomplished something. Think each one through in your mind and write two to three pages on the details of each experience. (Check back to your work history exercises in chapter 12.) What were you doing? Whom did you do it with? How did you do it? How did it turn out? What were the rewards? Get the job or experience clearly back in your mind. Then move through the checklist as in step 3, checking skills you used and double-checking ($\sqrt{}\sqrt{}$) skills you felt best about.

Step 5. Now you will be asked to make some judgments on the basis of your reflections. It may be difficult to do this, especially if you are currently in a job in which your best skills aren't being used. Do it this way. The checklist is divided into seventeen clusters or boxes of similar skills. By looking at your circled and double-checked boxes we want you to determine your top three to five clusters of skills—physical skills, communication skills, managing skills, performing skills. Be sure to rate the clusters or boxes of like skills instead of individual skills, e.g., physical skills instead of just traveling skills. Make a note in the notes section of the checklist which are your significant clusters.

Step 6. Now compare your circled and doubled-checked skills with those of the other rater(s). Talk to them in person if possible about their choices. Is there any consensus? If they checked areas you didn't, would you agree with their assessment? Does it change your top three to five root skill clusters? Make other notes in the notes section.

Group A— Realistic Things

	Your Rating					Notes
	Overall impression √ Most enjoyed ⊘ 10 skills	Present job √, √√	Previous job or experience #1	Previous job or experience #2	Previous job or experience #3	Other's view (10–15 checks)
1. Physical Skills	1	2	3	4	5	6
Using coordination and agility						
Outdoor—tennis, running, hiking, biking, camping, skiing, fishing						
Indoor—exercising, swimming, basketball, racketball, dancing						
Caring for plants, animals, farming						
Traveling, navigating skills						
Other:						
2. Mechanical Skills						
Designing, shaping, composing objects and machines						
Setting up equipment, adjusting equipment, repairing, controlling						
Assembling, building with precision, operating						
Lifting, balancing, moving, selecting tools						
Washing, cleaning, tending						
Cooking, crafts (woodworking, needlework)						
Other:						

Group B—
Investigative Data

	Your Rating					Notes
	Overall impres-sion √ **Most enjoyed** ⊘ **10 skills**	**Present job** √, √√	**Previous job or experi-ence #1**	**Previous job or experi-ence #2**	**Previous job or experi-ence #3**	**Other's view (10–15 checks)**
1. Learning Skills	1	2	3	4	5	6
Sensing, feeling, active involvement						
Observing, reflecting, perceptive of others						
Reasoning, abstract thinking, using logic, data						
Experimenting, piloting, testing						
Estimating, assessing others						
Other:						
2. Decision-making Skills						
Clarifying problems						
Researching, surveying, analyzing, diagnosing problems						
Testing out ideas, troubleshooting						
Reviewing, critiquing, evaluating, choosing, inspecting (ideas)						
Other:						

Group C—Artistic Data

	Your Rating					Notes
	Overall impression √ Most enjoyed ⊘ 10 skills	Present job √, √√	Previous job or experience #1	Previous job or experience #2	Previous job or experience #3	Other's view (10–15 checks)
1. Creative Skills	1	2	3	4	5	6
Imagining, intuiting, predicting						
Innovating, creating new ideas, experimenting						
Synthesizing, developing models, applying theory						
Perceiving shapes and design						
Other:						
2. Artistic Skills						
Sensitivity to beauty						
Using facial expression, voice						
Using symbols, visualizing, composing (music, poetry, photography)						
Designing visuals, fashions						
Directing productions						
Other:						

Group D—
Social People

	Your Rating					Notes
	Overall impres- sion √ Most enjoyed ⊘ 10 skills	Present job √, √√	Previous job or experi- ence #1	Previous job or experi- ence #2	Previous job or experi- ence #3	Other's view (10–15 checks)
1. Communication Skills	1	2	3	4	5	6
Speaking clearly, effectively						
Writing—reports, letters, memos						
Writing—promotional, creative, editing						
Reading—comprehension, speed						
Translating, explaining						
Other:						
2. Instruction Skills						
Coaching, informing, leading, facilitating groups						
Designing educational materials						
Creating learning environments, events						
Illustrating theories and principles through examples						
Other:						

continued

Group D—Social People (continued)

	Your Rating					Notes
	Overall impression √ Most enjoyed ⊘ 10 skills	Present job √, √√	Previous job or experience #1	Previous job or experience #2	Previous job or experience #3	Other's view (10–15 checks)
3. Human Relations Skills	**1**	**2**	**3**	**4**	**5**	**6**
Using counseling skills—empathy, rapport, patience, understanding						
Caring for, nursing, soothing others						
Managing office activities, atmosphere						
Negotiating, representing, advocating						
Other: **4. Mentoring Skills**						
Listening and questioning others, reflecting, guiding, reviewing						
Diagnosing others, evaluating feelings, giving feedback						
Developing others, coaching, forecasting, encouraging, motivating						
Sharing responsibility, problem solving, team building						
Other:						
5. Consulting Skills (used in indirect reporting relationships only)						
Giving ideas, clarifying procedures, developing rapport						
Informing, advising, assisting, guiding, persuading others						
Conferring, diagnostic, discussing, resolving, cooperating						
Recommending alternatives, following through, evaluating						
Other:						

Group E— **Enterprising People**	Your Rating					Notes
	Overall impres-sion √ Most enjoyed ⊘ 10 skills	Present job √, √√	Previous job or experi-ence #1	Previous job or experi-ence #2	Previous job or experi-ence #3	Other's view (10–15 checks)
1. Leadership Skills	**1**	**2**	**3**	**4**	**5**	**6**
Initiating activities, ideas						
Organizing time, self-direction						
Planning changes, anticipating problems						
Solving problems, using alternatives						
Risk taking, inspiring						
Other:						
2. Managing/Supervising Skills						
Setting goals and standards, assigning tasks						
Organizing others, coordinating						
Planning, developing, organizing ideas						
Designing projects, procedures, timetables						
Evaluating progress, choosing alternatives, troubleshooting						
Implementing policies, assigning responsibilities						
Evaluating performance of individuals						
Other:						

continued

Group E—
Enterprising People
(continued)

	Your Rating					Notes
3. Persuading Skills	**Overall impres-sion √ Most enjoyed ⊘ 10 skills**	**Present job √, √√**	**Previous job or experi-ence #1**	**Previous job or experi-ence #2**	**Previous job or experi-ence #3**	**Other's view (10–15 checks)**
	1	**2**	**3**	**4**	**5**	**6**
Influencing others, selling						
Developing trust, rapport						
Motivating others, coaxing						
Developing arguments, plotting, choosing strategy						
Managing conflict, reconciling, arbitrating						
Flexibility, stamina, follow-through						
Other:						
4. Performing Skills						
Performing, acting, using humor, spontaneity						
Modeling						
Public speaking, reading, telling stories						
Playing music, singing, dancing						
Competing at sports, games						
Other:						

Group F—Conventional Data	Your Rating					Notes
	Overall impression √ Most enjoyed ⊘ 10 skills	Present job √, √√	Previous job or experience #1	Previous job or experience #2	Previous job or experience #3	Other's view (10–15 checks)
1. Detail Skills	1	2	3	4	5	6
Keeping deadlines, details, accuracy						
Accepting responsibility, executing						
Making contacts, arrangements, brokering						
Organizing records, classifying, filing, processing						
Clerical skills, office machines						
Other:						
2. Numerical Skills						
Inventorying, classifying						
Using computational, statistical abilities						
Financial record keeping, appraising, projecting						
Managing budgets, money, allocating resources						
Other:						

Write down your top three to five cluster areas (for example, detail skills, leadership skills, performing skills, learning skills, instruction skills, mechanical skills).

Top skill clusters or boxes

1. _____
2. _____
3. _____
4. _____
5. _____

Next, check at the top left-hand corner of each page to find out which group of skills the cluster is in; A—Things: Realistic; B—Data: Investigative; C—Data: artistic; D—People: Social; E—people: Enterprising; F—Data: Conventional. Write the appropriate letters next to your skill clusters.

Group of skills represented A–F

1. _____
2. _____
3. _____
4. _____
5. _____

Are there any reoccurring themes in your checklist, like creative themes, people themes, being-in-charge themes, independence themes, numbers themes, organization themes?

Themes: _____

   Enter your top three to five root skill clusters in Box 15 on your Excursion Map.

Now that you have looked in depth at your root skills, we will move on to the second part of the analogy, the soil, which we call our survival skills.

15 Survival Skills

Survival skills are like the soil in which the tree grows and flourishes. The soil needs to have the ingredients for growth, and the tree needs to be receptive to growth (acclimatized). For example, an evergreen tree in a tropical soil would not flourish, because the mix of elements is just not right for the tree and the weather conditions are not appropriate.

Your survival skills are the traits you have and can use to help you not just to survive but to thrive, like intuition, patience, and curiosity. Surviving means knowing what you need and what you can get from your environment in order to grow. Selecting an organization in which you can plant your root skills, and thus grow and flourish, requires that you make a good definition of that proper soil. Survival on the job is linked to the best fit possible between you and your work environment.

In order to survive you must be able to read yourself and your environment. *These perceptive skills are so important that they are most often the prime factors in hiring, firing, demotion, and promotion.* You can spend months finding out which ones of your root skills are strongest and which you are really interested in using, only to be caught short by another set of factors—the mix of you and your environment. Many environments or organizations reward certain survival skills. You will be much happier in an environment that accommodates your best style.

CASE STUDY

Tom went sailing through the life- and career-renewal experience, really pinning down lifestyle changes and root skills. He concluded that he definitely needed a job change and promptly started interviewing. He did a good job of sorting out which skills he wanted to use and impressed the interviewers, and he landed a good job in just a few weeks. But after the first day of his new job, he decided that he was going to quit! What could possibly have happened? The people he was to work with, his co-workers, were clearly not his kind of people. These were things he'd never thought to ask about in the interview. A lesson well learned! (He didn't quit, but instead started thinking about his next job change and made some constructive changes in the present situation.)

People who have a good sense of their survival skills have the best chance of becoming inventurers—because they can choose more accurately the places where they will and will not be happy. Many of us will take the first new option or job or individual or experience that comes along, just to ease the strain, fill time, or get out of limbo and feel better.

Your *single most important* survival information is your knowledge of your learning style. Review your learning style profile on page 94. This is the way in which you process and learn new information in your environment. You can work well with people who have other learning styles if you can be somewhat versatile (use other styles) and appreciate the differences in styles. You will survive well if you capitalize on your most enjoyed style and blend it with the styles of others when you work as a team.

It is sometimes difficult to read yourself and your work climate. It takes wisdom to perceive the whole, to perceive essential relationships. The wise person is one who is able to "discern essential relationships" in a work environment, to be able to make the best decisions possible, as early as possible. Of the relationship between wisdom and knowledge, Ram Dass has said:

We would like to train for wisdom, not knowledge. And what we are training for is knowledge, because we can measure it. But knowledge is not convertible into human happiness and well-being. Wisdom is, because wisdom is learning how to live in harmony with the world.

LEARNING STYLES AND SURVIVAL

Each learning style has its positive and negative traits. Look at the strengths listed for your style, note the phrases that have meaning to you; then consider the following chart. It shows the typical reactions that different learning styles exhibit in different situations.

	Starting a new job	Approaching a career discussion with boss	Managing others
Enthu- siastic Learner	Meets co-workers. Gets the office look- ing friendly. Finds the lunchroom.	Talks with 3 or 4 friends about their ideas re career, is open to boss's ideas. Has general idea in mind of what he wants. Lets the deci- sion evolve; goes with the flow. Uses people environment as main criteria for job satisfaction.	Prefers face to face discussion. Brain- storms for ideas. Likes flexible dead- lines. Sets up a friendly, social atmo- sphere. Rewards spontaneity.
Imagina- tive Learner	Tours the office. Knows who's who. Gets a feel for the environment. Asks questions, observes.	Asks someone how his career discussion went. Listens to tapes on career man- agement. Prepares ideas, questions about careers in ad- vance. Thinks of how boss's mood will af- fect her strategy for discussion. Thinks of learning and creativ- ity as part of job sat- isfaction.	Prefers agendas, memos in advance. Outlines ideas with pros and cons. Pre- fers smooth, stress- free relationships. Rewards creative re- flection.

continued

continued

	Starting a new job	Approaching a career discussion with boss	Managing others
Logical Learner	Reads the manual. Finds out the rules. Looks at the organizational chart. Reads the annual report. Organizes desk and files.	Completes all career paperwork. Reads books on career management. Has lists of questions about all possible options. Completes work line for past ten years, projecting into the next five years. Gives boss a list of questions in advance. Thinks of technical expertise as job satisfaction.	Prefers written reports, well organized. Likes written ideas with back-up information on all of them. Wants clear understanding of roles, and harmony. Rewards competence.
Practical Learner	Finds out who does what, and where the power is. Finds problems to start solving. Gets a good assistant to file and organize.	Figures out where he wants to be when. Plans strategy with key people, including boss. Collects ideas about careers from a seminar on career management. Gives herself a goal and deadline. Thinks of problem solving as job satisfaction.	Prefers verbal summaries of ideas or one-page summaries. Welcomes list of ten ideas with best ones marked, with reasons. Likes direct conflict resolution. Rewards problem solving.

1. Put yourself in the same position on this learning-style profile as where you are in your learning style profile on page 94. Next put your boss, co-workers, spouse, and children on the grid.
2. What are the strengths of your learning style? How are others' strengths different?
3. What insights have you gained for dealing with other learning styles in work/home settings?

Learning-Style Profile

Enthusiastic	Imaginative
Practical	Logical

4. What is your level of flexibility, your ability to shift learning styles depending on the situation? (check one)
   ☐ Extremely flexible, sometimes wishy-washy
   ☐ Very flexible, generally shift to cope in diverse situations
   ☐ Patterned, change only if required by authority figure
   ☐ Stuck, unable to leave my comfort zone

   My closest friend/colleague tells me my level of flexibility is _____ .

Another part of your survival package is made up of your personal qualities and communication skills, the subject of the next exercise. Here's your chance to be a little clearer about the qualities that contribute to your survival skills. Have some fun with this and share it with the members of your inventure network.

Personal Qualities Exercise

Step 1. Complete this exercise quickly, without thinking too much about each item.

Step 2. For each of the following items, circle the number that best describes the degree to which the statement fits you.

Step 3. Have someone else complete the scale independently, reflecting the way he or she sees you. When both ratings are complete, proceed to steps 4 through 8 at the end of the list.

1. Listening ability	Low	1	2	3	4	5	High	(p)
2. Level of flexibility	Low	1	2	3	4	5	High	(s)
3. States meaning clearly	Low	1	2	3	4	5	High	(t)
4. Level of perseverance	Low	1	2	3	4	5	High	(s)
5. Understands someone else's meaning	Low	1	2	3	4	5	High	(t)
6. Avoids interrupting	Low	1	2	3	4	5	High	(p)
7. Level of energy	Low	1	2	3	4	5	High	(s)
8. Tolerance of pressure	Low	1	2	3	4	5	High	(s)
9. Initiates comments or suggestions	Low	1	2	3	4	5	High	(t)
10. Gets others to express ideas	Low	1	2	3	4	5	High	(p)
11. Risk preference	Low	1	2	3	4	5	High	(s)
12. States feelings to others	Low	1	2	3	4	5	High	(t)
13. Awareness of others' feelings	Low	1	2	3	4	5	High	(p)
14. Level of confidence	Low	1	2	3	4	5	High	(s)
15. Acceptance of feedback	Low	1	2	3	4	5	High	(p)

16. Level of inner peace, calm	Low	1	2	3	4	5	High	(s)
17. Tactfulness	Low	1	2	3	4	5	High	(p)
18. Trustfulness	Low	1	2	3	4	5	High	(p)
19. Cooperativeness	Low	1	2	3	4	5	High	(p)
20. Tolerance of differences and others' opinions	Low	1	2	3	4	5	High	(t)
21. Ability to overcome shyness	Low	1	2	3	4	5	High	(s)
22. Seeks close personal relationships	Low	1	2	3	4	5	High	(p)
23. Level of insight	Low	1	2	3	4	5	High	(s)
24. Influence on others	Low	1	2	3	4	5	High	(t)
25. Acceptance of affection	Low	1	2	3	4	5	High	(p)
26. Level of curiosity	Low	1	2	3	4	5	High	(s)
27. Constructive reaction to conflict	Low	1	2	3	4	5	High	(t)
28. Level of self-awareness	Low	1	2	3	4	5	High	(p)
29. Level of enthusiasm	Low	1	2	3	4	5	High	(s)
30. Versatility	Low	1	2	3	4	5	High	(t)
31. Seeks appropriate solutions	Low	1	2	3	4	5	High	(t)
32. Ability to meet deadlines	Low	1	2	3	4	5	High	(t)
33. Avoids monopolizing conversations	Low	1	2	3	4	5	High	(p)

Key: (t) items focus on task-oriented or problem-solving skills.

(p) items focus on relationship or people-oriented skills.

(s) items focus on personal style.

Step 4. Compare your ratings with the other person's.

Step 5. Which characteristics in the list are your three to five strongest? (scores of 5)

Step 6. Where do you need most improvement?

Step 7. Using the key, summarize your areas of greatest strength and weakness—task, people or personal style.

task (t) _____ people (p) _____ personal style (s) _____

Step 8. Suggest one way you could improve.

 Enter your three most outstanding personal qualities in Box 16 on the Excursion Map.

WORK ENVIRONMENT

The following questions focus on working-condition preferences, patterns of interaction, tolerances, and priorities. Answering these questions will help you not only survive in a work environment, but also succeed in job interviews. Personnel people tell us that successful candidates for jobs know what they want and what kind of an organization is the right place for them. Life and career renewers frequently tell us, "I want to work with people." That's about as descriptive as saying, "I want a job I will like." After all, morticians work with people too! Working through the following list of questions should help you arrive at more exact impressions of your preferred work environment.

Work Environment Preferences Exercises

What would ideal working conditions consist of for you? Sometimes it helps to think of the worst environment you've been in or can think of and note the elements present. Then think of your preferred working conditions.

	Preferred
Geographic areas	_____
General area (suburb, city, rural)	_____
Organization size (500+, 50–100, 10 or less, alone)	_____
Physical space (outdoors, indoors, private, open, office, plant)	_____
Dress norms (business attire, casual, uniform)	_____
Hours of work (9–5, flextime, part-time)	_____
People (personalities, backgrounds)	_____
Supervision (close and warm, hands-off, challenging, laid-back)	_____
Responsibility (how much, for whom, manage others or self)	_____
Style of work (alone, small group, team, large group)	_____
Other (benefits, parties, bonuses, parking)	_____

How much is environment a factor in your job satisfaction?

0% _____25% _____50% _____75% _____100% _____

Get feedback from someone who knows your work (a boss or co-worker). Ask them to say how and under what conditions you function best at work. Show them the list of work-environment criteria, but not your answers. Compare your ideal working conditions with the "Why do I work" exercise on page 136. Do you seem consistent in your values and your environmental needs?

> Enter your most important working conditions in Box 17 of the Excursion Map.

16 What Species . . . ?

Now let's look at the tree from another perspective. The species of tree you are is the subject matter, or special knowledge, you have acquired: the field you're in, your college major, the product you sell, or service you render. The world has usually identified you according to your species and labeled your work or title accordingly. Here are some examples:

Mental retardation: therapist, teacher

Law: lawyer

Manufacturing: engineer, manager

Education: teacher

Accounting: accountant

Automobiles: mechanic, salesman

Dentistry: dentist

Gerontology: therapist, social worker

Humanities: writer, researcher, teacher

Foreign languages: translator, teacher

Wood products: logger, carpenter

Chemical dependency: therapist, researcher

Psychology: psychologist

Computers: programmer, engineer

Insurance: insurance agent

Personnel: personnel officer

Plant biology: biologist

Preschool teacher

Architecture: architect, draftsman

Radio/TV: producer, announcer

Marketing: researcher, manager

Politics: politician, speech writer

You can usually identify knowledge or subject matter because it has a language built around it. We call it jargon. Educators don't understand engineers; biologists don't speak "legalese." It is important to have content or subject knowledge, because that's where we put our root skills to work. We learn the subject matter in school or in advanced training and put that knowledge to work in a discipline or a field by using our root skills. When we leave that area or career, we shed our work-content focus, but carry with us our same root skills to our next job or career.

CONTENT KNOWLEDGE

Many organization careers start out in a technical or functional area where a person is expected to master a certain content. Some people discover as they experience the work world that they have strong interests and are highly motivated for a certain kind of work or content area (finance, marketing, human resources, law, data processing). As these people progress they may find that if they are moved into other content areas they are less interested or satisfied. They build much of their satisfaction around the "content," the technical or functional area itself, and develop increasing skill within that area.

For others, mastering a particular function or content is simply a stepping stone to a higher rung in the organization. It is an opportunity to experience an area or learn a skill that they need for future assignments.

For some managers in organizations, often the function they are managing is more important than the management process itself; they clearly prefer the content of the work to management per se. They see themselves in their careers more in terms of their specialty. It is for this reason that "dual ladders" (management and technical) or dual career paths have been created in many organizations.

In most organizations, the largest group comprises people focused on their technical or functional competence. They are the craftspeople who want to become better and better at their craft. They are the real base of competence for the organization.

Thus, many of us build our sense of identity around the "content" of our work (e.g., the salesperson who specializes in a certain line, the manager for whom the function is most important, or the technical specialist or expert in any area). Often this means that they would not give up that area of work even if they had to sacrifice future career growth to remain in it. They will remain with the organization only if it continues to provide opportunities for growth in their area of expertise.

Content Knowledge Exercise

Answer the questions below regarding the importance of content knowledge to your work needs.

1. What did you concentrate on in school? Why did you choose those areas? How do you feel now about having chosen those areas?

2. What were your "knowledge or expertise" ambitions when you started your career? After graduation what were your objectives? Did you have any career aspirations/fantasies in school? Have you realized those ambitions?

3. As you look at your work life, can you think of times that you really enjoyed the work itself—the content? What did you especially enjoy about it?

4. How would you describe your current occupation or work to others? What is it you really do? What is the "content" you work with? Is it intrinsically interesting?

5. Have you ever refused a job or promotion? Why or why not?

6. As you look ahead in your career, do you want to sustain your special interests in later career stages? How will you avoid becoming content-plateaued or obsolete?

7. Are there other content areas in your organization that you have an interest in pursuing? Outside your organization? What are the barriers that keep you from exploring them further?

 Enter your most important content knowledge areas in Box 18 on your Excursion Map.

If you are unhappy with your job but basically content with the type of work you do, concentrate on finding better but similar jobs. If your discontent comes from the work itself, your goal is to find and move into a more suitable area or field. If you've found a satisfying career situation, stay with it, enjoy it, do it superbly. But consider that ongoing career planning is a fact of life today. Lifelong learning and development have become a necessity as technological change and global competition eliminate or restructure millions of jobs each year. People who assume that an organization will take care of them forever are often sharply awakened by technological change, mergers, or competitive reorganizations that leave them under- or unemployed.

One of the most important elements in career/life planning is to

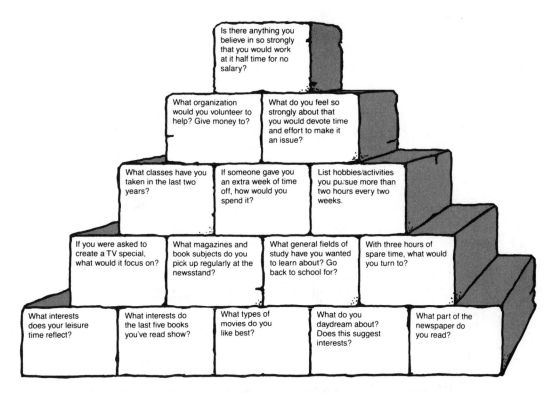

Figure 16.1. *Your pyramid of interests*

decide the areas of interest where you would be motivated to put your skills to work especially in your community or for leisure and renewal activities. All interests do not need to be pursued on the job. Having outside interests keeps us more in balance and more interesting. In fact, some people come more alive through their hobbies than through their paid work. Others find a way to utilize their interests through their work. Either way, it is important to know what our interests are. Unless you are interested in something you will see no way to put your skills to work.

Your Interests Pyramid

Interests are sometimes difficult to think about, so we are going to attack the subject from several angles. On the pyramid in figure 16.1

are a number of questions relating to interests. We use the pyramid to give you a chance to build your levels of interest on one another and figure out which are most important.

Step 1. Answer the bottom level first, then the second, third, fourth, and fifth. Write your answers in the boxes.
Step 2. Go over all the levels and circle any interests that reappear.

   After completing the exercise, answer the following questions:

1. What are your consistent interests?

2. Are most of your interests related to people, data, or things?

3. Were you surprised at your consistent interests? Why? Why not?

4. Summarize the kinds of problems, issues, people, products, etc., you believe you are interested in and with which you would like to do more, as a way of balancing or renewing yourself?

IIII➡ Enter your repeated key life interests in Box 19 of your Excursion Map.

17   You Only Go Around Once

Suppose you could enclose all the information you have gathered to date in a magic envelope and send it to us and we could tell you the ideal lifestyle or job for you. If we could do that, we'd have solved the biggest career problem of all time.

First, there is no ideal job, since all jobs have some aspects that are part drudgery. Second, there is no magic way to take all of our abilities, skills, and interests and link them to a job. There are more than likely a number of career areas or jobs that might fit. But all is not lost. There are several exciting things you can do to get a better perspective or handle on your lifestyle and your career.

Everyone goes about the change process a little differently. You have your own learning style, your own way of taking risks, your own sense of timing, and your own personal contacts. Our past experiences with other people indicate that when you're ready, you'll "do it," but that readiness is an individual thing. For some, it means getting sick and tired of the present circumstances; for others it's making a change at the peak of success. Some people need friends to give them a swift kick; others change as a result of life events. Boredom moves some; too much activity convinces others. Everyone who's reported a change cites different "straws" that broke their backs or different reasons for change. Here's what some people have done on their way to becoming inventurers.

- A thirty-three-year-old woman elementary school teacher elected to leave teaching several years ago to identify business opportunities. With three other colleagues, she started a computer software business. It continues to be an exciting venture. But in her heart she has always known she wants to work directly with people and the decisions they make for their lives. Currently she is doing some volunteer work for a women's center and planning to go back to school for further study in women's issues, spirituality, and counseling. She says "As I grow, I am struck by the beauty and power of choice."

- Bill was with a large banking corporation that was experiencing downsizing. After twenty-three years at the bank, he lost his position as vice-president of marketing and sales. Devastated, he thought his life was over. As he began to evaluate where he had been and what he had done, it became clear to him that his stress level had been too high. He decided he would be in direct marketing services but not with a bank and not in a large corporation. He had always been intrigued with the health-care field. Through networking and interviewing he gathered the data he needed. He is now a director of marketing for a hospital.

- Cory was an operations manager for a mid-sized corporation. He decided he wanted to spend the last third of his career working more for himself and being more directly rewarded for the results he produced. As a manager he felt he had good persuading and selling skills because he frequently had had to present his ideas to the management committee. He also had extensive knowledge of automated equipment. Today he is a sales rep for an automated–office equipment firm. Because of his operations background, he also meets regularly with the product development team.

- Becky worked in accounting departments at a number of businesses. She would easily get bored and move on to another company. She frequently felt stuck. Until her early thirties she did not recognize that she was setting up her own barriers. She said, "In naming and facing the issues of my life, a new world opened. I'm amazed at the road I see as I look back." Becky is talking about the discoveries she made when she realized she was an adult child of an alcoholic. Through a painful inner journey, she began to realize why she had felt stuck. She learned to like herself and to accept her high level of intelligence and her special gifts of analyzing and problem solving. She had always enjoyed math. She returned to school, became a CPA and worked for several companies. The jobs were very satisfying, but she thought she had excellent skills for managing people. Becky recognized if she could become a chief financial officer, her people skills could be utilized. She started her search in businesses where she had previous experience. At the age of forty-two she became the CFO of a land title company.

- A twenty-eight-year-old college recruiter decided to call it quits with his job. He leaped at a chance to sell recreational products, because his interest was so high in the area and his skills included sales. He failed to realize that the amount of travel and socializing involved did not suit his personality. It took him another several months to locate a more desirable position within the recreation industry. Now he is much happier and more satisfied.

- A successful writer had advanced to the position of editor of a magazine, only to find that she was competent but not totally interested in the administrative role. After much deliberation, she found a good and trusted colleague who agreed to share a job. They wrote a job-sharing proposal to her supervisor. It was so convincing that after a lengthy discussion, it was accepted as a pilot. It has been working successfully for several months, and now, in addition to her administrative duties, she can still write.

- A bank president going through a midcareer reassessment decided to make a lifestyle and job change. She wanted to live in a small town and be comfortable financially. She conducted personal research for nine months, talking to everyone she knew who could help her. She made the switch by buying a prosperous bank in a smaller town near a metropolitan area. She lives on a lake and rides her bike to work—and feels ten years younger.

- A sixty-five-year-old woman retired from her administrative job and decided to take advantage of her curiosity and love for learning. She enrolled at a local college (at senior citizen tuition rates) and started work toward her B.A. degree in literature. It'll take her eight years, but she loves every minute of it. She also walks two miles every day. Her friends think that she's getting younger, not older.

- A psychiatric nurse who worked mostly with children decided after several years that he wasn't suited to the conditions—the hospital environment, the emotional intensity, the hours, and the line of command. He decided to make an abrupt career switch, because otherwise he might never do it at all. He took a wild chance at real estate, which had been mentioned to him as an independent career (his primary work value!). He plunged right into it, took the ups and downs in stride, and organized his own counseling approach to selling homes. Now he's developed a program for prospective home sellers and buyers that's based on his previous work experience. He's never been so excited about work. He works nine months and travels three.

- A corporate secretary wanted to further her career within the company. She asked her supervisor to send her to seminars and in-service training sessions to increase her skills with people and management. Soon she was recognized for her initiative and skill and was assigned to a special project. She performed so well that she was slowly eased into a staff function in the education division. Along the way, she acquired a B.A. degree so that she would be ready for the next advancement. She's now a successful instructor and supervisor.

- A couple who were both pleased with their jobs decided to make some lifestyle changes; she was mostly responsible for the child-care and housekeeping duties, while her husband did all the home maintenance. They realized it was because neither was experienced in the other's roles. She took classes to learn home-maintenance skills, and he learned to cook. After some initial awkward attempts, they found they enjoyed the wide range of new skills and activities. They also shared the child-care responsibility. He has even taken the child with him on some work trips to broaden his experiences with parenting.

- As a result of a life/career-planning course, two thirty-five-year-old attorneys dissatisfied with their law firms got to talking about their philosophies of work and life. They both felt strongly about certain specific ways of operating and they decided during the course to go into private practice together. After much lengthy discussion and lots of searching, they opened an office together. They both say it's the best thing they've ever done, even though it's still in the experimental phase.

- A fifty-year-old male who was successful in his career but not sufficiently challenged got very interested in children with heart problems as a result of a grandchild's tragic illness. He devoted time and energy to publicity and campaigns and found numerous rewards in volunteer activity. He felt that he was being of service to others and to his own family, and continuing this work became one of his retirement goals.

- Two roommates decided that they greatly disliked their jobs and that they wanted to move to a city they both loved in another state. One of them could readily get a job there as an accountant, but the other would have more difficulty. They took a vacation there together to look around and make contacts. As luck (or fortuitous planning) would have it, a friend of a friend needed temporary help. They moved a month later, and both started working. Eventually, the temporary job collapsed, and one roommate had a period of unemployment. By agreement, this time was used to get their house in order and for the unemployed roommate to look for more meaningful work. A few months later, a professor friend quit his job, and it was exactly suited to the roommate. They now say it was one of the biggest and best risks they've taken.

- One forty-six-year-old man had become quite skilled in his computer-design job, but had become stale because of the sameness of his daily routine. He did a thorough self- and work-assessment and decided to propose a change to his manager. He proposed a team-project approach on the next work assignment, and after some negotiating, the manager decided to try the idea. It worked much better than expected, and now the man has other proposals in mind to keep his job interesting.

- A recent college graduate in advertising decided that his job was not totally satisfying, but that he wasn't ready to change. He decided to start a small operation on the side, through mail-order sales. He designed and produced hobby supplies for matchbook collectors (a need he saw around him) and is small but successful. He has met a challenge for himself personally—and this is just the first step!
- An attorney was practicing successfully, but not really living out her dream. For years she'd studied and applied herself and she was really getting weary. She decided to live out her dream before it was too late. She boarded a freighter in Los Angeles and is now proceeding around the world—her lifelong dream. She plans to return to the practice of law near a wilderness setting.
- A thirty-two-year-old educational-program planner loved his job but was ready for a new challenge, something that would really test his skills and abilities. He decided to apply his skills to a long-term interest—music! He now gets paid to design unique musical experiences for corporations, conferences, reunions, department stores, shopping centers, and airlines.

These examples are designed to show you that the conclusion you reach as a result of this chapter may be a very obvious one, or it could be earth-shattering at first. It may be that you'll make a lifestyle change, an attitude change, a relationship change, a project change, a job change, a career change, or several of the above—or no change at all.

The end result we expect is that you will know the excursion process (the steps) of life and career renewal in order to achieve balance and satisfaction in your own life. If you know the process, you can go back and use it when you're ready. Growth occurs with change, and you can decide to create change. It is sometimes called a creative crisis. But life is too short to postpone. When will you decide to decide?

If you are ready and willing to put it all together and become an inventurer, then let's get on with it. Several steps are involved, which you can do at your own speed.

18 Step 1: Your Excursion Map

Go back and complete the boxes through Box 19 on your map that you have left undone. If necessary, talk with other people to get help.

The Excursion Map

	Personal qualities	Work environment	Content knowledge
	Box 16 (p. 172)	Box 17 (p. 173)	Box 18 (p. 178)

	Life-balance circles	Life space location	Learning styles
	Box 6 (p. 67)	SMall town WATER RURAL HILLS/MOUNTAINS Box 7 (p. 82)	Practical Box 8 (p. 98)

	Root skill clusters	Financial needs	Work values
	Box 15 (p. 164)	Box 14 (p. 146)	Box 13 (p. 138)

	Dialogue insights	Inventure network	Life themes
	Box 5 (p. 58)	Role Model Granny Mentor Nancy Intimate Sheryl Box 4 (p. 55)	Relationships Work Box 3 (p. 42)

"The inventurous life"

"A decision"

"Limbo"

Life interests

Box 19 (p. 180)

Life Purpose Statement

curity
cognition
AMily

Box 10 (p. 112)

"Searching time"

Life dream/goal

Box 11 (p. 121)

Inventurer's Life/Career Conclusions:

Lifestyle needs

_____
_____
_____
_____ Box 20 (p. 192)

Work/career needs

_____
_____
_____
_____ Box 21 (p. 194)

Brainstorming options

_____
_____
_____
_____
_____ Box 22 (p. 206)

Promoters   Deterrents

_____
_____
_____ (p. 224)

Coping style

_____
_____
_____ (p. 229)

Fantasy

DLIFE
sition
f-searching
ritual

Teaching
Coaching
Farming
Voluntary Work

Box 1 (p. 12)

"Triggering events"

"Life plateau"

START HERE
on your life
inventure

19　Step 2: Conclusions

Life and career choices reflect a whole variety of conscious and unconscious needs and impulses.

Chance, accident, and serendipity are at the very heart of life. The inventuring process does not automatically eliminate these factors. It cannot deliver you from the necessity of guesswork or of using your best hunches or your intuition. The process does, however, attempt to ensure that you are giving due consideration to the key life/career decision factors.

You have expended much time and energy on this process. What really is the end product?

- It may be the realization that you are a unique individual with a special pattern of talents, skills, style, values, and interests.
- It may be making specific decisions about your future.
- It may be sharing insights and decisions with spouse, friends, or work colleagues.
- It may be using your Excursion Map to brainstorm new lifestyle or workstyle options.
- It may be discussing your insights with your boss or other people in your organization.
- It may be doing nothing but, perhaps, deciding to accept or enjoy your present situation and review this process again at a later date.

Implementation—taking action—is a difficult step for many people. Often we don't act because we are unsure of the trade-offs we'll need to make. Is the change worth it? What will I need to let go of?

The inventuring process is designed to help you determine your life/work preferences and to think through your options. The next few exercises are designed to help you summarize your present situation. Regardless of your current job or career, your future decisions will be easier if you have a clear summary of your life and work satisfactions and dissatisfactions.

Open your Excursion Map in front of you and review the lifestyle sections (Boxes 1–11). Underline, make further notes, and use your intuition. Take each box one at a time and look for what it implies regarding life or career. How important is the conclusion or insight—is it of great, moderate, or minor importance? After reviewing your map, complete the Lifestyle Summary Exercise below. As a supplement to this, try letting a significant person in your life answer the same questions about you. Be sure, though, that both of you approach the questions thoughtfully and with complete candor.

There are no wrong answers. However, there should be an honor code. Put down the real answers. Take enough time thinking about the questions to really get the honest facts about you.

Lifestyle Summary Exercise

Read through the following items. Indicate your level of satisfaction with each area by circling A, B, C, D, or E, where A is the lowest degree of satisfaction and E is the highest.

To review your responses, plot your scores on the worksheet below by connecting the dots with a line. Now choose a different-color pen and circle where you want to be with each item. Where there is low satisfaction, try to identify some reasons for this. Look at the places where there are the largest gaps between where you are now and where you want to be.

The summary is intended to help you quickly analyze your lifestyle. These questions aren't the only ones you should be asking yourself. Whether or not your answers indicate a need for growth or change, it's always a good idea periodically to assess where you are and set revised goals.

Analyzing your current satisfaction level (recognizing that no life is perfect) should provide the basis for life planning and growth.

Where are the largest gaps between the present and the fulfilled you?

_____

_____

_____

 Enter your conclusions in Box 20 of your Excursion Map.

Now that you've completed the Lifestyle Summary, what does it mean? You've probably already sensed the meaning and have gotten real benefit from just thinking about and answering the questions. The major advantage is to give you some structure for thinking about the various areas of your life. The total score is not particularly significant. But take a hard look where you were less than satisfied. These questions can be very important growth tools.

The Lifestyle Summary

	Degree of Satisfaction		
	None	Some	Very Much
1. Do I feel an appropriate balance of internal and external success?	A B	C D	E
2. Have I accomplished some of my life dreams?	A B	C D	E
3. Am I an interesting person? Do I like the person I've become?	A B	C D	E
4. Am I satisfied with the depth of my spiritual life?	A B	C D	E
5. If I were to die today, would my life have made a difference?	A B	C D	E
6. Do I feel as if I'm growing and alive at this stage of my life?	A B	C D	E
7. Do I take time most days to be alone to think, meditate, or reflect?	A B	C D	E
8. Am I having fun in life?	A B	C D	E
9. Am I satisfied with my health, energy, and vitality?	A B	C D	E
10. Do I have a financial plan that will work now and in the future?	A B	C D	E
11. Am I satisfied with my family relationships?	A B	C D	E
12. Do I have close personal friends?	A B	C D	E

The Lifestyle Summary

	Satisfaction Level				Satisfaction Level		
	None	Some	Very Much		None	Some	Very Much
	A B	C D	E		A B	C D	E
1. Balance	• •	• •	•	7. Alone	• •	• •	•
2. Dreams	• •	• •	•	8. Fun	• •	• •	•
3. Personhood	• •	• •	•	9. Health	• •	• •	•
4. Spiritual	• •	• •	•	10. Money plan	• •	• •	•
5. Purpose	• •	• •	•	11. Family	• •	• •	•
6. Growth	• •	• •	•	12. Friends	• •	• •	•

Workstyle Summary Exercise

Lay your Excursion Map in front of you and review the workstyle sections (Boxes 12–19). Underline, make further notes and use your judgement. Take each box and look for what it implies or suggests about your life and career. After reviewing your map, complete the Workstyle Summary Exercise below. Read through the following items. Indicate how satisfied you are with each item by rating it from A to E.

Plot your scores on the worksheet that follows by connecting the dots with a line. Use a different color pen to indicate where you would like to be with each item. Where there is low satisfaction, try to identify some reasons for it.

Analysis of your current satisfaction—recognizing that no job is perfect—should provide the basis for job planning, redesigning, or change.

Where are the largest gaps between the present and ideal you? _____
_____
_____

 Enter your work conclusions in Box 21 of your Excursion Map.

The summary is intended to help you quickly analyze your current work situation. These questions are not the only ones you should be asking yourself. Whether or not your answers indicate a need for growth or change, it is always a good idea periodically to assess where you are and set revised goals. It is highly probable that staying up-to-date can only be achieved by deliberately projecting yourself into changed conditions.

Workstyle Summary

	Degree of Satisfaction		
	None	Some	Very Much
1. My knowledge in this area/field	A B	C	D E
2. My root skills	A B	C	D E
3. My interest in this kind of work	A B	C	D E
4. My current income	A B	C	D E
5. My chances to grow and develop new skills	A B	C	D E
6. My participation in decisions about my career	A B	C	D E
7. My impact on the organization	A B	C	D E
8. My fit with the environment	A B	C	D E
9. My relationships with the people I work with	A B	C	D E
10. My general motivation for this kind of work	A B	C	D E
11. My future in this area/field	A B	C	D E

	Satisfaction Level				Satisfaction Level		
	None	Some	Very Much		None	Some	Very Much
	A B C D E				A B C D E		
1. Knowledge	• • • • •			7. Impact	• • • • •		
2. Skills	• • • • •			8. Environment	• • • • •		
3. Interest	• • • • •			9. Relation	• • • • •		
4. Income	• • • • •			10. Motivation	• • • • •		
5. Growth	• • • • •			11. Future	• • • • •		
6. Participation	• • • • •						

20 Step 3: Getting Feedback and Ideas

Inventuring is an ongoing process of knowing what your priorities are and knowing how to talk about them. It is a matter of both preparation and opportunity. Writing answers to the questions in this book and drawing one's own conclusions are not sufficient.

Throughout the book, many of the exercises and the Excursion Contracts have suggested that you work with a partner to get further feedback and insights. Hopefully you have done this and selected someone with whom you can be open and frank about past and future career issues.

Many people report that a spouse is a good partner. Even if the spouse is not working or fully involved in a career, the feedback can be essential to sorting out priorities.

It is also helpful to select a boss, manager or peer with whom to further test out your thinking. If you're uncomfortable with your boss, peers in the same organization can work well if you feel comfortable with one another.

CAREER PLANNING FOR PEOPLE IN ORGANIZATIONS

Most career planning sessions succeed if both manager and employee are well prepared. An excellent way for an employee to prepare is by completing the Excursion Map and the Lifestyle and Workstyle summaries. How you choose to communicate your priorities is up to you.

Development Planning

Many organizations require their managers and supervisors to formulate a development plan annually for each employee. The inventuring process can serve as valuable part of the planning process.

Having A Career Discussion With Your Boss

Inventure Interview   Your boss is an important person to incorporate into a career dialogue. It's important to know how your boss sees you. Your boss can provide feedback on your skills, structure development opportunities into your current job for you, and speak well of you to other people in the organization.

Your career plans don't stand alone. You must also be concerned with your boss's plans. You can't guess what they are for either your job or for the entire function or department. So ask. Only then you can plan to cope with the differences, negotiate to redesign your job description, or take some other action.

Whatever the outcome, remember a conference with your boss to discuss your career growth is one way of managing your career effectively. You will have done your homework responsibly!

But remember, bosses come in all different styles. Many bosses fear that a career discussion will raise uncomfortable issues or raise false expectations. Many have never had useful career coaching themselves and lack the skills and confidence for handling the process.

You may surprise your boss by asking—but you will arouse his or her interest too! To stir interest, try . . .

"I've completed *The Inventurers* and established a career map for myself. I would like to talk to you about it. I'm also interested in your perspective on my career and where you see me heading."

With this question, be ready to discuss your Excursion Map or Lifestyle/Workstyle summaries and conclusions.

Once the time and place of your meeting is scheduled, you should spend time preparing for the meeting by completing the Inventure Interview Worksheet.

Inventure Interview Worksheet

1. I have initiated a meeting with _____
   (Manager)

   on _____ specifically to discuss _____
      (Date)

   _____

   _____

2. Check the quality of your working relationship with your manager:
   ☐ Poor   ☐ Okay   ☐ Good   ☐ Very Good

3. Is my manager really interested in my career growth?
   ☐ Yes   ☐ No   ☐ Not Sure

4. Have I ever discussed my career goals with my manager?
   ☐ Yes   ☐ No

5. If yes, what happened? My manager was:
   ☐ Supportive and helpful
   ☐ Supportive but not much help
   ☐ Uncomfortable with the discussion
   ☐ Not supportive
   ☐ Disinterested and not supportive
   ☐ Other: _____

   _____

   _____

6. What do I think my manager's reaction to my Inventure Map and Conclusions will be if I choose to share it? _____

   _____

   _____

7. If we should disagree on my strengths, interests or future career options, how will I most likely respond? _____

   _____

   _____

Inventure Interview Summary

The "next steps" I am considering relating to my career plans are:
☐ To stay where I am; I'm satisfied with my present career situation.

☐ Not to make any decisions now and review this process again on

_____
(Date)

☐ To redesign my present job to make better use of my strengths and interests.

☐ To pick up/polish up these skills:

_____

_____

☐ To adjust my career to fit my lifestyle.

☐ To change jobs.

Explain: _____

_____

_____

☐ To complete these on-the-job development activities:

_____

_____

_____

☐ Other: _____

_____

_____

Barriers

If where you want to be in three years, one year or six months is a long way from where you are now, you will need to examine your present life and working situation for barriers. Some typical barriers are:

- The need for more education
- Lack of experience in particular kinds of work
- Concerns about the risks involved (e.g., financial security)
- Geographic preference
- Lifestyle balance (increased time, travel, pressure)
- No visible job openings for your next step
- Having to take a salary cut
- Only lateral or downward movement possible

- The need for more skills
- Endless other possibilities . . .

Do you see any barriers to getting what you want?

Further Questions

Some questions that may be useful in exploring a new job or career situation in your current organization include:

Regarding the Job Itself

1. What major tasks are involved?
2. What root skills are needed to perform each task?
3. Approximately what percent of the time will you spend on each task?
4. What time constraints do you have to work within (pace, deadlines, etc.)?
5. How many hours per week do people holding similar jobs work?
6. What percent of the time will you be working alone?
7. Have you interviewed your potential colleagues? What are these people like? What percent of the time will you be with them?
8. How much freedom will you have in deciding how to perform the job?
9. What's your boss's style? How good a coach is she?
10. How is performance measured in this job?
11. What type of salary and other rewards are available, given what level of performance?
12. Very specifically, what type of advancement opportunities are available to you? Who makes the decisions regarding promotions?

Regarding the Organization

1. How old is this part of the organization? What are the key events in its history?
2. How large is this part of the organization (people, assets, sales volume, net income)?

3. Where does it have plants or offices?
4. What important technologies does this area use?
5. What are the major parts of the organization and how are they structured?
6. Does the organization have any important traditions?
7. How does the overall management style and environment feel?
8. What are this area's plans for the future?

BRAINSTORMING

Brainstorming is another way to generate feedback and ideas. After you have studied your Excursion Map, brainstorming can generate options—alternative ways to achieve your goals.

Getting all the ideas you could ever use is really not as difficult as it may appear. By simply knowing where you want to go, you are at once in a position to find many, many ways to get there.

If you want ideas you've got to ask people the right questions.

Brainstorming is a widespread problem-solving method. Generating alternatives is its basic purpose. It is practical because any group of three persons can quickly learn to generate scores of ideas in very short periods of time. The originator of brainstorming in his book *Applied Imagination*, Alex Osborn, lays down four requirements for all who participate in a session:

- Defer judgment—so criticism does not come forward
- Freewheel—hang loose
- Tag on—don't wait for an idea; make another one out of the last one given by changing it in some way
- Quantity is wanted—don't hold back for a minute

One of the characteristics of most great thinkers is the ability to be comfortable with the approximate, and the seemingly irrelevant. It's disturbing to realize that most of the characteristics of creative thinking (uncertainty, wrongness, confusion, excitement) are frowned upon in our culture.

The problems easiest to solve usually belong to the other person. The moment a problem becomes "our problem," psychological barriers are set up which make it seem more complex.

Following that line of thinking, you might benefit by asking someone totally unfamiliar with the problem for ideas. The more casual the acquaintance, the more likely it is that you will be given a unique view. Close friends are often not as useful when it comes to unique views because they assume nearly the same personal feeling toward your problem as you do.

First you might decide what action you want to take as a result of your inventuring.

- Make lifestyle adjustments
- Make major lifestyle changes
- Start working or going to school
- Stop working or going to school
- Change work environment
- Change workstyle and assignments
- Change jobs within the same organization
- Change job by moving to another organization
- Change career

Here is an expanded list of specific options to get you thinking about your own. You will think of several other options, too.

1. Options within the working setting
   a) Set new goals and standards
   b) Assess my attitude
   c) Tackle a new project
   d) Participate in in-service training
   e) Participate in a reading program
   f) Pursue additional education
   g) Change the emphasis of responsibility
   h) Propose "on-loan" assignment to another part of the organization

    i) Rearrange work environment

    j) Seek trial work on a different project

    k) Join team project or task force

    l) Make a recommendation or proposal

    m) Consult with another department or division

    n) Arrange to work with people you enjoy the most

2. Options outside the work setting
   a) Creative moonlighting—second job
   b) Part-time employment—present or new job
   c) Capitalize on a hobby, physical activities
   d) Volunteer activities, community, professional—get active in clubs, organizations, church, politics
   e) College classes or degree—present or new subject area

3. Options for career or lifestyle change
   a) Partial career switch—your present skills in a new area
   b) Total career switch—new skills, new area of work
   c) Stop to rethink—travel, relax, do nothing, unemployment
   d) Sabbatical
   e) Move to a new geographical location
   f) Leave of absence
   g) Retire—on time or early—or decide not to retire at all
   h) Dual career—share a job with someone
   i) Switch roles with spouse

Now you need a little help from your friends. You want as many ideas as you can possibly get from people as to what you can do, given your Excursion Map information. You'll need good brainstormers, because you want lots of options, even if you end up choosing only a couple.

Even if you want to make a small environmental change, it's worthwhile completing this exercise. You can get much more specific suggestions after you get broader ones. If you're making lifestyle or job changes within organizations, you'll want to gear the brainstorming more specifically after you get the broad perspective. Do this individually or in a small group, but *be sure to do it*. Form an inventure group or a personal board of directors for assistance on your excursions. It is vital that you get several creative options both in lifestyles and careers so you can start the next step in the process. Encourage people to dream and to be farfetched, to get outside the ruts of conventional thinking. You can reality-test later.

You'll find that it's easiest to think of options when you blend specific pieces of information. Form a simple equation (similar to the examples that follow). Put the parts of this equation on large sheets of paper and tape them up on the wall.

Have your brainstorming partners look at the different blocks on your Excursion Map and think of activities, lifestyles, and careers, using new combinations of your skills and interests. Root skills are the key to the equation; without them, you'll have no grounding. Then you'll want to *apply* your root skills to something that truly *interests* you, that you feel some passion about. Options will be all the imaginable ways your root skills and interests can be combined. There are several ways to approach this; each varies with the kind of information you've collected and your style.

Have your brainstorming partners call out as many options as possible—they can be silly, farfetched, or seemingly unrealistic. You're not going to be held to any of the ideas. But you need a starting point. It is *imperative* that you have enthusiastic, interested people do this, or you could get bogged down here. Get at least twenty ideas.

When people give you ideas to put into the hopper, listen and write them down, but do not start telling the brainstormers why you can't do the ideas, or don't want to, or why someone else won't let you. Practice open-mindedness and free expression. We'll get to realities next. This approach will lead to lots of possibilities.

Here are a few brainstorming ideas that other groups have developed for one another. They were told to really dream, for out of dreams emerge ideas and motivation!

Inventure Equation

Root skills 1. 2. 3.	×	Interests, issues, life goal, on-the-job interest, fantasies, or basic life values	=	Options

| Consulting and traveling | × | Sports, independent lifestyle | = | Consultant for ski areas. Farfetched? Not so! He's doing it! |

| Writing, mechanical skills, creative talent | × | Anthropology, reading, photography | = | Creator of photo essays for magazines; editor of anthropology-related publication. She's learning! |

| Research, physical activities | × | Wilderness, camping, flying plane | = | Research director for camping-equipment company, pilot who tests camping gear. |

| Administration, managing | × | People, travel, French | = | Administrator of travel-incentive organization; sets up trips around world; travels to foreign countries free! |

| *Mentoring, creative talent* | × | *Youth counseling, crafts* | = | *Counseling youth in drop-in center (volunteer basis); works with arts/ crafts.* |

If you want to be more systematic in your brainstorming, use the following formula and come up with at least twenty options for your life, your present work, or future work. The box numbers refer to the boxes on the Excursion Map. This example is from a nursing manager in a metropolitan hospital who wanted to renew her career.

Root skills	+	Interests	+	Special Knowledge	+	Life/Work Values	+
Box 15		**Box 19**		**Box 18**		**Box 9,13**	
managing		holistic health		nursing-oncology		expertness	
persuading		hiking		psychology		variety	
leadership		fitness				services	
communicating							

Work Environment	+	Life Dream/Goals	+	Life Purpose	+	Fantasy	= Options
Box 17		**Box 11**		**Box 10**		**Box 1**	
team leader		balance in life/work		help eradicate cancer		retreat center	
small group of real "pros"		develop management skills		holistic clinic			
little supervision required		willness education					
informal communication							

Options (on-the-job plus future)

Find a mentor in management to teach skills

Take wellness courses

Get involved in "visions" program in the hospital

Independent study in nonprofit organization management

Get involved in P.R. area of hospital

Work one night a week in holistic clinic

Manage hospice

Camp nursing

Go to retreat center on summer vacation

Get into new development area of hospital or into outpatient area

Join a professional organization of nurses interested in holistic
  health

Attend wellness conferences

Corporate nurse—wellness emphasis

Set up fitness program for hospital personnel

Now it's your turn. You might want to use a larger piece of paper to
add more information.

Root skills	+	Interests	+	Special Knowledge	+	Life/Work Values	+

Work Environment + Life Dream/Goals + Life Purpose + Fantasy = Options

Brainstorm

 Enter your brainstorm options in Box 22 of your Excursion Map.

Now step back and choose three to six items on the list that you think are reasonably good ideas. Get more specific ideas from your network of supporters: whom do they know who is doing these activities, where can you get more specific information.

The trick is to make sure that your best and most enjoyed skills were selected and that your most valued interests, issues, and subjects were explored. The broader your experience has been, the more opportunities you'll have to choose from. So volunteer, take extra assignments, go to classes—expand your horizons. Sometimes you can use exactly the same skills—writing, designing, managing, teaching—but apply them to an area you are more interested in, such as social service, plants, recreational products, travel, philosophy. Or you can use the exact same job skills but transfer them to another project within the job or organization. If you are interested in expanding your skills on your present job, plan carefully, then approach your supervisor, dean, manager, or project director about it. The options are endless. The rest depends on you.

There are several other resources in addition to you, your friends, and mentors that you can use to assist you in putting it all together.

- Other workbooks and interest inventories—see the bibliography
- Reference material, for example, *Dictionary of Occupational Titles, Occupational Outlook* handbooks
- Professional career counselors
- Action-oriented course or support group
- Internships and related experiences

None of these resources is a substitute for doing this work on your own with your inventure network, but they can provide additional information that reinforces your decisions.

Some changes will be small, others large. You may find that what you want to do will take longer than you thought. Well, change always takes more time than we think it will. Expect any substantial change to take a year. That seems like a long time; but remember, you'll be working on the change the whole time. As time goes on, your first ideas will change somewhat, and the opportunities that arise may alter your goals a little. You are experiencing what are called trade-offs. You get part of what you want, but give in somewhere else (sort of like negotiating the purchase of a house or car!). What you must keep in mind are the things or qualities or ingredients you want most in your life and what you're willing to do to obtain them. It all evolves once your mind is focused. Also, starting with small changes leads inevitably to bigger ones. It's catching! Don't be surprised when your friends get the bug too! Also, expect ups and downs. The important thing is not that you have ups and downs, but how you handle them.

21 Step 4: Reality Testing

With this step in the excursion process, you are beginning to reality-test your self-assessment against life and career options in the real world. You've decided to work for balance, growth, renewal, or a change. Depending on your learning style, perhaps your initial efforts in this process were primarily introspective. All new data are evaluated in terms of compatibility with what you know about yourself. But now is the time to activate options or paths that you may wish to explore. Most of us have many options to choose from. You must identify where and how you can best utilize the unique dimensions of *you* that make up *your* Excursion Map.

None of us begins this active exploration process as a blank page. We have had significant role models, mentors, and intimates who have influenced our views of various career paths. To pursue new directions without our own input of facts and reality testing could easily lead to a future of frustration. Reading all the literature and seeking advice from professionals in a number of fields still probably won't produce an absolute certainty about direction. The most useful reality testing is direct contact or experience. There is no substitute!

Several years ago we saw an Australian film called *Walkabout*. This provocative film is about a young Australian aborigine on his walkabout—a six-month solo excursion test in the wilderness, a rite of passage that precedes his acceptance into adult society. The movie was thought-provoking in that it presented an analogy, or blueprint, for a challenging and appropriate process of reality testing.

The young native in the movie had to demonstrate that he had acquired the awareness and skills necessary to make him a contributor and a survivor in his society. By contrast, we are often faced with only safe paper-and-pencil tests of our awareness and skills, and often they are far removed from the actual experiences we will have in real life. Often we do not allow ourselves to apply what we know in strange but real situations. And yet, is it not clear that what really matters is not so much what we know about, but what we feel, what we stand for, and what we can do and will do?

In our opinion the walkabout is a useful analogy to our exploration of our own life and career options. The walkabout analogy suggests that your "reality testing" should be measured against a number of criteria:

1. *Experiential*. Your reality tests should be real rather than simulated; we must get out and experience—taste, touch, feel, smell, hear— the options we are exploring. One experience of breaking through the confines of your perceived limitations, one telephone call, one risk, is the seed for further growth and is worth your full attention.

2. *Challenging*. Your excursions should challenge and excite your capacities as fully as possible, urging you to consider every obstacle you put in your own way as a barrier to be broken through. Reality tests are challenges to your daring and skill in an unfamiliar environment, challenges to explore and to express your own imagination in some exciting form.

3. *Self-directed*. Your excursions should be challenges you choose for yourself. The major challenge is in making decisions. In primitive society there are few choices; in ours there is a confusing array of options in lifestyle and work. Happiness depends on your ability to make appropriate choices for yourself. The competition is with yourself, not with others. The satisfaction is in the recognition by others of what you have proved to yourself: "This is what I can and will do!"

It is through walkabout experiences that we are able to choose options to work for. Fantasy becomes reality. We learn to trust our own experiences, judgments, and information and to rely less and less on what we perceive to be the judgment of society.

Society often fears the inventurer—people like you who explore options that follow the dictates of your own conscience. Reality testing will make some people around you uneasy—spouses, friends, parents, employers. The uneasiness or conflicts are the result of the fear we have of facing ourselves.

What kind of "triggering event" will have the power to transform your energy into action? What would be an appropriate and challenging walkabout for you?

Using a variety of resources will increase your knowledge of options and provide the reality testing needed to translate your interests into action. The first step is organizing yourself.

First of all, to reality-test your ideas it's necessary to scrap a number of well-entrenched convictions. This, you'll quickly discover, is more easily said than done, for initially you'll only half believe in the effectiveness of strategies. You'll find yourself raising all sorts of objections, which is another way of saying that long-held beliefs and values are being threatened. Try not to make judgments, however!

Let's look at reality testing in terms of the active job search. Some of you are probably mumbling under your breath, "It's a waste of time to organize an active job search. Everyone knows jobs depend on who you know and on luck—being in the right place at the right time." No one can argue with that! But there are a number of factors influencing a successful job hunt that you can control. Why not maximize your luck by focusing your energy on those factors?

THE FOCUS PROCESS

The active career-hunting systems in our society are, at best, haphazard and casting-about processes. In spite of the fact that all of us are involved in the job hunt at some time in our lives, very few of us really know how to go about it in a way that works to our maximum benefit.

Ninety percent of the population goes about the job hunt in a random, disjointed manner. Perhaps it's because people don't know what they're looking for to begin with. Or perhaps it's because they don't know how.

It's not our intention to focus on the job-hunting process. Our intention is to ask the tougher and deeper questions that all of us experience in our life and career journeys. *The Inventurers* addresses career preparation, on-the-job adjustment, underemployment, organizational adaptation, midcareer renewal and change, and retirement.

The Focus Process is a series of strategies to assist you in planning a systematic job search. It is based on the following points:

1. The key ingredient to the search is complete information and experience gathering. There is no substitute!
2. Employers hire solutions to problems. Jobs are really problems that need solving.
3. Employers offer jobs based on abilities that you communicate to them to solve their problems. Thus, after the vital information gathering, 70 percent of the search depends on "becoming a candidate" and effectively presenting yourself as a solution to the problem.

The steps to implement these strategies are:

F Functional brief
0 Occupational research
C Creative exploration
U Unique interviewing
S Supportive follow-up

Let's look briefly at each step.

Before you begin the external job-hunting process, you must be sure you have completed, to the best of your ability, the internal self-search process. If you don't know what you want and who you are, job hunting will be like trying to buy raisins in a hardware store.

So as you begin the active Focus Process, use the information on your Excursion Map to complete this excellent job criteria worksheet provided to us by one of our colleagues, Betty Olson. She says it is the most effective tool she uses.*

Job Criteria Worksheet

This is a summary of what *you* are looking for in a job. Be sure your most important criteria can be met.

1. *People*: What kinds, how many, type of interactions. (Work Conditions Preference Exercise, Box 17, page 173; Personal Qualities Exercise, Box 16, page 172; and Learning Styles, Box 8, page 98)

2. *Physical Surroundings*: Indoors, outdoors, windows, lighting. (Box 17, page 173)

3. *Atmosphere*: Flexible attitudes, chance for promotions, warm and supporting, competitive, etc. (Box 17, page 173; Box 12, page 133)

4. *Responsibility*: How much, for whom, progressive responsibility for tasks and/or people. (Box 17, page 173; Box 12, page 133)

5. *Work values*: List your top six work values. (Box 13, page 138)

————————
Used with permission of Betty Olson and Associates. Copyright © 1978, revised 1986.

6. *Personal values*: List your top three personal values from the Life Values Profile and your life purpose statement. (Box 9, page 104; Box 10, page 112)

7. *Root skills*: List your top three to five root skill clusters from the Root Skills Checklist Exercise. (Box 15, page 164)

8. *Survival skills*: List your top six personal qualities from the Personal Qualities Exercise. (Box 16, page 172)

9. *Content knowledge*: List all the content knowledge you believe you have. (Box 18, page 178)

10. *Interests*: List your top three interests related to work and your top three non-work-related interests. (Box 19, page 180)

11. *Personal*: Type of clothing you would like to wear, preferred form of transportation to work, preferred housing location, salary needed, hours, vacation time. (Box 17, page 173)

The Functional Brief

A functional brief is one of your major tools in the active job search. Your brief translates your excursion map into a format that makes sense to a potential employer. Often called a "résumé," your brief states your case for you. It differs from a classic résumé in several respects. First, it is functional. It is based on what you can offer and how you can solve the problem of a potential employer. It is not a laundry list of everything you've ever done, in chronological order. Second, it is brief. Like a lawyer's brief, it makes a highly persuasive case for you in about one minute or less—which is the average reading time allotted to this sort of tool.

Employers are busy people who often spend many hours reading the résumés of aspiring employees. There are probably as many opinions concerning the "perfect brief" as there are employment specialists. The bibliography contains books that will teach you, very capably, to develop your own résumé or brief. Job hunting experts such as John Crystal, Richard Bolles, Robert Wagner, Richard Lathrop, Bernard Haldane, and Howard Figler have developed excellent approaches to this subject. In conjunction with the assistance they offer, the following strategies may also help:

1. Create your own unique formula for a brief; don't follow any formula blindly.
2. Develop one now and keep it on hand; it tends to bolster your self-esteem even if you don't really need a job right now. Besides, writing it when you're feeling best about yourself will result in a better brief.
3. Consider including these sections in your brief:
   a) *Objective*: The level and function (not job title) you seek. Focus on the likely needs of the employer.
   b) *Qualified by*: Support your objective by showing how the scope and effect of your past experience can help solve the employer's problem. Use action verbs, e.g., managed, directed, sparked, accomplished, developed, saved.
   c) *Education*: Education recedes in importance as an employment factor over time. Treat this section accordingly.

d) *Other*: Personal traits, interests, civic activities, honors, licenses, publications, professional memberships, etc. Focus on the needs of the potential employer.

Keep in mind that the primary purpose of your functional brief is to get you in front of a live person for an information-gathering or job interview.

Occupational Research

Armed with a functional brief that focuses on your objective and your strongest attributes, you should then gather information on the *occupational fields* that meet your objective, the *organizations* within those fields, and the *individuals* within those organizations. We mentioned earlier that the key is complete information gathering and experience. Stay in the information-gathering phase. The minute you say that you are seeking a job—*slam!*—you see doors shut. If you ask for information, however, people will open doors for you. We all like to share information with "allies"—people who are interested in the same subjects we are, or, better, even interested in us.

Sound difficult? It's not really. Try it. Go back and briefly review chapter 9. Occupational research is accomplished best in your own unique learning style. Consider these options:

- Call or visit people in your inventure network. Ask for information, but be sure you don't ask for jobs.
- Scan the Yellow Pages of your phone directory to get an overview of a field of interest. Visit or tour several of the organizations that seem most interesting.
- Visit your local library. Libraries are excellent resources for occupational research. The library is jammed with relevant occupational reading on all three levels—occupational fields, organizations, and yes, even individuals (*Who's Who in Business*).
- Set up an "inventure search team" of a personnel professional, librarian, employment agent, and mentor. Map out a step-by-step information-gathering plan and checkpoints for completion.

The purpose of occupational research is to narrow your focus down to a manageable handful of possibilities that truly interest you. At the same time, you're trying to get a glimpse of the problems that those occupations, organizations, and subsequently interviewers are most concerned with. The next step is to explore these in more depth.

Creative Exploration

You've finally settled on several organizations that really interest you. Now, how do you get in to see the person(s) in a position to hire you? This step calls for all the courage and energy you can muster!

Numerous surveys have been conducted by the Department of Labor as well as private organizations to determine the most effective methods of making the "job connection." Typically the studies show that in an average cross section the population, consisting of one hundred people, here is how the "job connection" was made:

1%—private agency	6%—school placement	48%—personal network
3%—public agency	24%—direct contact	13%—combination of the other six
5%—want ads		

We don't like those data any more than you probably do. But experience backs up those figures very solidly. Common sense would indicate that you should spend roughly three quarters of your active job-search efforts on the informal exploration system—contacting people and places directly and seeking assistance from your network. Richard Bolles's excellent book, *What Color Is Your Parachute?* discusses this in more depth.

Unique Interviewing

There is quite a difference between interviewing for information and interviewing for jobs. The former is designed to explore work areas, interests, people, skills, climate, and values of various jobs or organizations. The job interview focuses on a specific job with the intent of becoming the best candidate if the match is right for you. Interviewing for information should be done prior to job interviewing. We will not focus on information interviewing because it is covered so thoroughly by Dick Bolles and others.

All of your efforts up to this point have been designed to open the door to a job interview. You must now rely on your performance in the interview to secure the position.

The job interview is an opportunity to match your skills and interests with *one* way of using them. In addition to convincing the employer that you are the best candidate to solve the problem, the interview should also help you determine if this is the best career path for you—it is a two-way situation.

Consider the interview in two phases:

Phase 1: Preparing for the interview
Phase 2: The interview.

Let's look at these phases separately.

Phase I: Preparing for the Interview

Only through planning and anticipating your interview performance can you present yourself in the most focused manner. The ingredients here are the same as those mentioned earlier.

Step 1. Find a comfortable position and talk yourself through the relaxation exercise (pages 78–79).

Step 2. Think about a potential or upcoming interview. Envision yourself in that interview.

  a) What is your image of yourself?

  b) What image do you think the interviewer has?

  c) How is the way you talk, walk, dress, act, and listen likely to affect the interviewer?

d) What type of image do you project in relation to your chosen area of work?

Step 3. Develop answers to each of these questions out loud in a "dry run."

a) Why should I hire you?

b) Why are you leaving your present situation?

c) What two or three accomplishments have given you the most satisfaction? Why?

d) In what kind of work environment are you most comfortable?

e) What do you know about our organization?

f) What major problem have you encountered and how did you deal with it?

g) What criteria are you using to evaluate the organization for which you hope to work?

h) What specific personal goals have you established for yourself in the next five years?

i) How long would you stay with us?

j) What pay do you have in mind?

k) What would you do to improve our operations?

l) What kind of relationship should exist between a supervisor and subordinate?

m) Tell me about yourself.

In preparing for the interview, use the following checklist:

Have I . . .

Yes	No	
____	____	Learned about the organization?
____	____	Learned about the work/job/problem?
____	____	Learned about the interview?
____	____	Decided which problems my skills can help solve?
____	____	Listed my questions?
____	____	Prepared a functional brief (to send before or leave with the interviewer after the interview)?

_____ _____ Listed my references?
_____ _____ Confirmed the appointment and time frame?
_____ _____ Scouted the "survival" environment?
_____ _____ Thought of my purpose going in?
_____ _____ Thought of my plan of action coming out?

At some point in the interview, the employer will ask if you have any questions. If she doesn't ask, be sure to take the initiative, early on, to ask yours. Specific questions you might consider listing ahead of time are the following:

1. Would it be all right if I asked you a few questions?
2. Would you mind describing the duties of the job for me?
3. What abilities do you need most (least) in people on this job?
4. What is the largest single problem facing you now? Is there a specific problem with [quality work, increased production, greater efficiency, lower waste in time, effort, materials]?
5. Could you tell me about the people I would be working with?
6. What are the primary results you would like to see me produce?
7. Do any factors prevent action along this line?
8. Have you had a chance to review my functional brief?
9. Did it raise any questions about my qualifications I can answer?
10. May I check back with you on [specify when]?

Phase II: The Interview

Interviewing styles vary considerably, but most involve a fairly even give and take. Flexibility is the key. You can relax and let things flow if you have prepared carefully before the interview. By doing your homework, you can actually make interviewing fun.

Several interview strategies might be useful to consider:

1. What learning style do you think the interviewer is? What type of information is that style most comfortable with?
   - *Enthusiastic learners* will like success stories, actual experiences, enthusiasm, inspiration.

- *Imaginative learners* will be interested in the way you relate to them, how interesting you are, how friendly you are.
- *Logical learners* will be interested in facts, prior experience, details about your skills, abilities.
- *Practical learners* will be interested in problems you've solved, accomplishments, results, new ideas you have.

2. Be alert to nonverbal clues. Fifty-five percent of the communication both ways will happen through nonverbal body language, 38 percent through the tone of what's said, and 7 percent through the actual words. Watch for clues to make sure you're on track.
3. Interviewers are more likely to hire you if they have the feeling that you understand *them* and *their problem*.
4. Don't assume that interviewers always know what they're looking for. They may be shopping! Clarify your position and expectations.
5. Make sure you have a purpose going in and a plan of action coming out.

Supportive Follow-Up

An interview can be lost in the follow-up. Follow-up is absolutely crucial, yet hardly anybody does it. We often assume that after the interview, we should sit back and wait. Remember, employers offer jobs on the basis of *abilities* you communicate to them. After the interview, you should have enough information to focus your efforts more. Ask yourself: *"What further information can I offer that will assist the interviewer in making the decision?"*

Send a thank-you note immediately, that day, not a typical note, but a *focused* one. Review your interview discussion, state any significant insights you gained, reaffirm your interest in the position, inquire about follow-up procedures, and confirm when you expect to hear results or about the next step.

If you are really focused, you might also consider sending a functional proposal as follow-up. Such a proposal might consist of the following elements:

1. Cover letter
   a) Review your interview discussion.
   b) State crisply the purpose of this proposal.
2. Background
   a) Describe the situation as the interviewer saw it.
   b) Highlight the specific problem you're most interested in applying your skills and abilities to help solve.
3. Proposal
   a) State your solution or how you would propose to solve the problem.
   b) Embellish your proposal with past accomplishments and/or specific illustrations.
4. Why you?
   a) Briefly review your qualifications.
   b) Refer to and/or attach your functional brief.
5. Benefits to the organization
   a) Project potential benefits to the organization from hiring you and implementing your solution.
   b) Cost to the organization—compare the potential benefits against the salary you would expect.

The focus process is designed to help you put yourself in that successful 10 percent of the population that knows what to look for, knows how to go about the active job search, and does so in a systematic manner. The results are startling! Almost everyone in that 10 percent gets a surge, a glow, a tingle, at the idea of uncovering options. Often these people get job offers in the information-gathering stages because they are efficient and impressive with their self-organization skills. The world does indeed stand aside for a person with a plan!

If you find that you need additional job-hunting help these books should be useful:

- Bolles, Richard. *What Color is Your Parachute?* Berkeley, Calif: Ten Speed Press, 1987.
- Lathrop, Richard. *Who's Hiring Who?* Berkeley, Calif: Ten Speed Press, 1977.

- Wallach, Ellen and Peter Arnold. *The Job Search Companion*. Boston: Harvard Common Press, 1984.
- Figler, Howard. *The Complete Job Search Handbook*. N.Y.: Holt, Rinehart & Winston, 1979.
- Jackson, Tom. *Guerrilla Tactics in the Job Market*. N.Y.: Bantam, 1980.
- Wegmann, Robert, *The Right Place at the Right Time*. Berkeley, Calif.: Ten Speed Press, 1987.

22 Do It!

By this time you have more ideas than you know what to do with. You look around you at other people who've made changes, and it looks so easy, but now that it's staring you in the face, it never looked so hard.

Here's the spot where a lot of people get stuck. All the subtle reasons for not doing things or making changes creep in and now take on immense proportions. It's inevitable! We're creatures of habit and cling to status quo. It's hard to change. It leaves us off balance temporarily. We're not sure of the results. We've never done it before. Limbo doesn't look so bad any more. Other people are involved. You can ask yourself two major questions to get a better perspective about this limbo time:

1. If not now, then when will I do it?
2. What's the worst thing that can possibly happen? (Many people say, "I could still be doing what I'm doing now!!")

Don't run away from or hide your fears and resistance. Face them head on and decide how you plan to cope with them. Don't be afraid to be afraid. Here's an example to get you started.

Coping with Change

In the following list, circle on the left all the factors that assist you in making changes (or a specific change); on the right, circle your favorite reasons for not making changes.

For change (promoters)

skills, motivation, a course, family support, self-confidence, someone's death, age, health, interests, experience, risk-taking ability, fulfillment, praise and encouragement, purpose, friends, energy, time, a mission, ideas, education, a shock, a role model, need for variety, a good offer, dissatisfaction, spouse, divorce, new life stage, support-group pressure, new challenge, opportunity, geographical move

Against change (deterrents)

lack of skill, no motivation or course, family responsibility, high expectations, no confidence, lack of money, need for security, seniority, comfort, too old/young, illness, no interest, lack of experience, no focus, too safe, no contacts, low energy, no time, lack of education, fear of failure, fear of success, fear of unknown, fear of commitment, low self-esteem, confusion

You have no doubt noticed the similarity in the two lists. You see, you can use anything as an excuse if you want to.

 Enter your most important promoters and deterrents in the space provided next to the Excursion Map.

List ways to overcome, modify, or challenge items in the right column by means of compromise, negotiation, creative alternatives, using resources in the left-hand column.

Look over the case studies in chapter 17 and talk to your inventure network about their suggestions. If you really want to do something, there's always some way.

Most people use money as the biggest block. If that's what you are doing, reread the chapters on money and sincerely put yourself to the test. Perhaps it would be more fair to give yourself some time and a plan for working out finances rather than shelving an idea because you can't afford it.

Family responsibility is another big reason for stagnation. But when you discuss change with your family, often they are very supportive after initial fears are voiced. You see, they'd rather live with someone who's doing more of what he or she wants to do and who is happy. You're not doing anyone a favor by "postponing" your life away for their sake. Test it out before you give up.

There are some additional factors to consider in making changes, based on your preferred learning style. Each learning style has both traits that hold us back from making changes and specific strengths that will help us to approach change in the most constructive manner. And that's how serendipity occurs. Serendipity is not magic, but rather a set of fortuitous events that happen when you are investigating what you really want to do and using your most comfortable style doing it! The following chart suggests some assets and liabilities users of each style will probably encounter.

LEARNING STYLES AND CHANGE

	Liabilities	**Assests**
Enthusiastic	No organization or goal setting	Gets others involved
	Too impulsive	Operates on intuition, "gut" reactions
	So involved, he becomes splintered	Takes risks with new experiences
	Loose ends are not always taken care of	Very active when motivated
	Becomes unbelievable to other people	Will talk to other people and get inspiration in process
	Changes jobs too quickly	May try several options

Imaginative	Afraid to change relationships	Will generate lots of options for change
	Creates conflict or hurts people, so stays the same	Observes how others have made the change
	No change results with all the efforts, just good ideas	Uses creative hunches, plays with ideas; fantasizes, can see images
	Security with status quo	Lets ideas integrate or come together before changing
	Won't be pushed	
	Waits too long for inspiration	Can wait for the best timing
Logical	Needs too much evidence before acting	Gathers relevant facts in logical order
	Too cautious, slow, methodical	Very organized
	Doesn't get involved with people	Reads books, looks at several resources or approaches
	Too bogged down in theory	Double checks
	Wants too many guarantees	Analyzes options, calculates probabilities
	Takes risks very slowly	Can map out on paper before jumping in
		Works well alone
Practical	Is incautious	Sees change as problem to be solved
	Lets task take precedence over people	Uses detective skills to get facts
	Impatient	Evaluates options, sets up trial situations
	Needs to control and do it alone	Sets goals and acts, doesn't get bogged down
	Doesn't listen enough to others	Works well independently

One other thing to keep in mind is that your most comfortable style can leave you just that—most comfortable. There comes a time when logicals have gathered enough information, analyzed most of the options, and must finally do something, act on it. Enthusiastic learners need to stop and figure out which of the many experiences they've had is worth pursuing further. Imaginatives must take initiative to test out some ideas. And practical learners need to sit back and reflect on their experiments to get a broader view of the activity. Each of us has more than one learning style at our disposal and this is the time they are most useful. And the more flexible you can be, the more you can capitalize on your styles.

Coping with uncertainty is called risk taking. The goal of an inventurer is to turn risks into adventures. The actual point of change, the turning point, is achieved only after collecting all of the resources and weighing the uncertainties. Some people can stand financial uncertainty far more easily than relationship uncertainty. Some people take physical risks more easily than risks with ideas. By using your main learning style to approach uncertainty (e.g., practicals seeing finances as a task or problem to be tackled on their way to a goal), once you get to the point of actually doing it or mulling it over afterward, it ceases to be such a risk. Logicals would probably analyze all options before plunging in; enthusiastics would most likely jump in and look later; practicals would take a risk only if it looked useful; imaginatives would observe how others have done it and pick the best way in time.

You probably learned how to cope with uncertainty in your family, and you are better at handling some risks than others. You've already rated your risk taking in the survival skills section. Now try to imagine how you and your parents would respond in the situations listed below.

Coping Style	How would I approach . . .	How would or did my parents approach the same risks?
• Financial risks Loss of job or job change Major purchases, risky investments Betting on sports events, races		
• Emotional risks Big disagreement between family members Divorce or separation Asking for love or affection		
•Intellectual risks Sharing original ideas Differing with others' opinions Reading and discussing subjects outside your area of expertise		
• Physical risks Trying new sports challenges Coping when in physical danger—storms, car accidents Recovering from illness		

1. Do you follow any of your parents' patterns? How? _____

   _____

2. What kind of uncertainties or risks are you best at coping with? ___

   _____

3. How can you consciously use your learning style to cope more confidently? _____

   _____

   _____

 Enter your best coping style (financial, physical, emotional, intellectual) in the space provided next to the Excursion Map.

Do It! Be an Inventurer

You have just completed what could be the most important process in your life. You may have discovered skills you never before knew you had, reviewed your life in a new way, felt the ups and downs of the change process, formed new inventure networks or rejuvenated old ones, established new goals and planned concrete ways to meet them, or made a decision to stay in your present lifestyle or job and put more energy into it. Whatever you've concluded at the end of the process, you are among the people who are on their way to becoming inventurers.

Here's something for you to think about. It was written by an eighty-five-year-old inventurer, and it speaks for itself.

Picking Daisies *

If I had my life to live all over again, I would pick more Daisies.
If I had my life to live over, I would try to make more mistakes next
   time,
I would be sillier than I have been this trip,
I would relax. I would limber up.

_____

* From *Mindstyles/Lifestyles*, © 1976 by Nathaniel Lande. Reprinted by permission of the publisher, Price/Stern/Sloan.

I know very few things I would take seriously. I would be crazier,
I would be less hygienic; I would take more chances;
I would take more trips; I would climb more mountains;
Swim more rivers, and watch more sunsets.
I would burn more gasoline. I would eat more ice cream and less
    beans.

I would have more actual troubles, and fewer imaginary ones.
You see, I am one of those people who lives prophylactically
And sensibly and sanely, hour after hour, day after day.

Oh, I have had my mad moments, and if I had it to do all over
    again,
I would have more of them; in fact, I'd try to have nothing else,
Just moments, one after another, instead of living so many years
    ahead.

I have been one of those people who never go anywhere without
    a thermometer,
A hot-water bottle, a gargle, a raincoat and a parachute.
If I had it to live all over again I would go places and travel lighter
    than I have.

If I had my life to live over again, I would start barefoot earlier in
    the spring,
And stay that way later in the fall. I would play hookey more,
I would ride on more merry-go-rounds. I'd pick more Daisies.

We urge you to make a decision at some point in your life (preferably
now) that you believe in yourself, your skills, your lifestyle options, and
your interests, and that life means juggling all those factors in different
ways for continual renewal. It never stops—even if you try to make it
stop.

Make a decision to join the other folks who are becoming inventurers—join the club. Inventurers are people who are taking charge and creating their own challenges to get themselves moving. More specifically, you are an inventurer if you are willing to take a long look at yourself and consider new options, venture inward, and explore. You are an inventurer if you see life as a series of changes, changes as growth experiences, and growth as positive. You are inventuring on life's excursions and learning about yourself as a result. You are willing to risk some disappointments in your quest because you are committed to a balanced lifestyle and to more than just making a living. You are part of a unique group of people who want to make a living work. If you have these qualities, you are an inventurer.

Make a decision. We encourage you, we challenge you, we dare you. And when you do, let us know what it is so we can share with other people your successes (see page 237).

Make a decision that your life is too short to let yourself be stopped by waiting, by postponement games, by ruts. Recognize the fact that you could cage yourself up indefinitely unless you act. There are four elements that each inventurer must keep in mind for life and career renewal success. With these you can get out of the CAGES you are in. And with those four elements we will close this book.

C Choices and options
A Aloneness
G Guts, courage
E Energy
S Support

Be an inventurer!

Appendixes

Appendix A: Inventurer Summary

Name _____

Address (optional) _____

    I have drawn the following conclusions after completing *The Inventurers*.

1. *Current lifestyle/career*

    _____ I have reviewed my lifestyle and am satisfied, happy.

    _____ I have reviewed my lifestyle and am making changes.

    _____ I have completed my career-growth proposal and met with my supervisor or mentor.

    _____ I have made changes in my current job.

    _____ I have reviewed my job and am satisfied

    _____ I have decided that it's too early to predict what will happen.

2. The most interesting part of the inventure process for me was:

3. Suggestions I have for other inventurers:

    Share your inventure story with us and send to: Janet Hagberg and Dick Leider, c/o General Books, Addison-Wesley Publishing Company, Reading, Massachusetts 01867.

Appendix B: Bibliography

Ardell, Donald. *Fourteen Days to a Wellness Lifestyle*. Mill Valley, Calif.: Whatever, 1982.

Baldwin, Christina. *One to One: Self-Understanding through Journal Writing*. New York: M. Evans, 1977.

Baldwin, Roger, et. al. *Expanding Faculty Options*. Washington: D.C.: American Association of Higher Education, 1981.

Bardwick, Judith. *The Plateauing Trap*. N.Y., AMACOM, 1986.

Beattie, Melody. *Codependent No More*. New York: Harper/Hazeldon, 1987.

Becker, Ernest. *The Denial of Death*. New York: Free Press, 1973.

Bennett, Hal, and Mike Samuels. *The Well Body Book*. New York: Random House/Bookworks, 1973.

Benson, Herbert. *The Relaxation Response*. New York: Avon, 1976.

Blotnick, Scrully. *Corporate Steeplechase*. New York: Facts on File, 1984.

Bolles, Richard. *The Quick Job Hunting Map*. Berkeley, Calif.: Ten Speed Press, 1975.

———. *What Color Is Your Parachute?* Berkeley, Calif.: Ten Speed Press, 1974. (Updated yearly.)

———. *The Three Boxes of Life*. Berkeley, Calif.: Ten Speed Press, 1978.

Bridges, William. *Transitions*. Reading, Mass: Addison-Wesley, 1980.

Byrd, Richard. *A Guide to Personal Risk Taking*. New York: AMACOM, 1974.

Campbell, David P. *If You Don't Know Where You're Going, You'll Probably End Up Somewhere Else*. Niles, Ill.: Argus, 1974.

Crystal, John, and Richard Bolles. *Where Do I Go from Here with My Life?* New York: Seabury Press, 1974.

Dass, Ram. *Grist for the Mill*. Santa Cruz, Calif.: Unity Press, 1977.

———, *The Only Dance There Is*. Santa Cruz, Calif.: Unity Press, 1974.

Diehl, William. *In Search of Faithfulness*. Philadelphia: Fortress Press, 1987.

Edwards, Betty. *Drawing on the Right Side of the Brain*. Los Angeles: Tarcher, 1979.

Elgin, Duane. *Voluntary Simplicity*. New York: William Morrow, 1981.

Erickson, Erik. *Life History and the Historical Moment*. New York: Norton, 1975.

———. *Identity: Youth and Crisis*. New York: Norton, 1968.

Ferguson. Marilyn, *The Aquarian Conspiracy*. Los Angeles: Tarcher, 1980.

Ferguson, Tom. *Medical Self-Care*. New York: Simon & Shuster, 1980.

Figler, Howard. *The Complete Job Search Handbook*. New York: Holt, Rinehart, and Winston, 1979.

Foster, Richard. *Celebration of Discipline*. San Francisco: Harper & Row, 1978.

———. *Freedom of Simplicity*. San Francisco: Harper & Row, 1981.

Frankl, Viktor E. *Man's Search for Meaning*. New York: Washington Square Press, 1963.

———. *The Unheard Cry for Meaning*. New York: Touchstone, 1978.

Fried, Barbara. *The Middle Age Crisis*. New York: Harper & Row, 1976.

Furniss, W. Todd. *Reshaping Faculty Careers*. Washington, D.C.: American Council on Education, 1981.

Gardner, John W. *Excellence*. New York: Harper & Row, 1961.

————. *Self-Renewal*. New York: Harper & Row, 1964.

Germann, Richard. *Job and Career Building*. Berkeley, Calif.: Ten Speed Press, 1980.

Glasser, William. *Positive Addiction*. New York: Harper & Row, 1976.

Goodman, Ellen. *Turning Points*. Garden City. N.Y.: Doubleday, 1979.

Gould, Roger. *Transformations*. New York: Simon and Schuster, 1978.

Hagberg, Janet. *Real Power*. San Francisco: Harper & Row, 1984.

Heilbrun, Carolyn. *Reinventing Womanhood*. New York: Norton, 1979.

Herzberg, Frederick. *Work and the Nature of Man*. Cleveland: World, 1966.

Holland, John L. *Making Vocational Choices—A Theory of Careers*. New York: Prentice-Hall, 1973.

————. *The Self-Directed Search*. Palo Alto, Calif.: Consulting Psychologists Press, 1970.

Jung, C. G. *Man and His Symbols*. Garden City, N.Y.: Doubleday, 1964.

Keen, Sam. *What to Do When You're Bored and Blue*. Wyden, N.Y.: 1980.

Kirby, Patricia. *Cognitive Style, Learning Style, and Transfer Skill Acquisition*. Columbus, Ohio: Ohio State University, National Center for Research in Vocational Education, 1979.

Knowles, Malcolm. *The Adult Learner: A Neglected Species*. Houston: Gulf, 1973.

Kolb, David. *Learning Style Inventory Technical Manual*. Boston: McBer and Co., 1976.

————. "The Experiential Learning Theory of Career Development." in *New Perspectives on Organizational Careers*, edited by J. Van Mannen, New York: Wiley, 1976.

LaBier, Douglas. *Modern Madness: The Emotional Fallout of Success*. Reading, Mass.: Addison-Wesley, 1986.

Lakein, Alan. *How to Get Control of Your Time and Your Life*. New York: Wyden, 1973.

Lande, Nathaniel. *Mindstyles/Lifestyles*. Los Angeles: Price/Stern/Sloan, 1976.

Lathrop, Richard. *Who's Hiring Who*. Reston, Va.: Reston, 1976.

Lecker, Sidney. *The Money Personality*. New York: Simon & Shuster, 1979.

Leider, Richard. *The Power of Purpose*. New York: Fawcett, 1985.

Leider, Richard, and James Harding. *Taking Charge: A Daily Self-Management Process*. Portland, Oreg.: Leider-Harding Publishing Company, 1981.

Leonard, Linda. *The Wounded Woman*. Boston: Shambhala, 1982.

Lerner, Harriet. *The Dance of Anger*. New York: Harper & Row, 1985.

LeShan, E. J. *The Wonderful Crisis of Middle Age*. New York: David McKay, 1973.

Levinson, D. J. *Seasons of a Man's Life*. New York: Ballantine, 1978.

MacDonald, Gordon. *Ordering Your Private World*. Nashville: Nelson, 1984.

————. *Restoring Your Spiritual Passion*. Nashville: Nelson, 1986.

Maitland, David. *Against the Grain*. New York: Pilgrim Press, 1981.

Maslow, Abraham. *Toward a Psychology of Being*. New York: D. Van Nostrand, 1961.

Miller, Arthur and Ralph Mattson. *The Truth About You*. N.J.: Fleming Revel, 1977.

Missildine, W. Hugh. *Your Inner Child of the Past*. New York: Pocket, 1963.

Myers, Isabel Briggs. *Gifts Differing*. Palo Alto, Calif.: Consulting Psychologists Press, 1980.

Newman, James W. *Release Your Brakes!* New York: CBS, 1977.

Nickles, Elizabeth. *The Coming Matriarchy*. New York: Seaview Books, 1981.

Nouwen, Henri. *Out of Solitude*. Notre Dame, Ind.: Ava Maria, 1974.

Olson, Tillie. *Silences*. New York: Dell, 1965.

Ornstein, Robert E. *The Psychology of Consciousness*. New York: Viking, 1972.

Paulus, T. *Hope for the Flowers*. New York: Paulist Press, 1972.

Peck, M. Scott. *The Road Less Traveled*. New York: Simon & Schuster, 1978.

Pelletier, Kenneth. *Mind as Healer, Mind as Slayer*. New York: Dell, 1977.

Peterson, Eugene. *Traveling Light*. Downers Grove, Ill.: Inter Varsity Press, 1982.

————. *Running with the Horses*. Downers Grove, Ill.: Inter Varsity Press, 1985.

Phillips, Michael. *The Briarpatch Book*. Los Angeles: Reed Books, 1978.

————. *The Seven Laws of Money*. New York: Random House, 1974.

Pirsig, Robert, *Zen and the Art of Motorcycle Maintenance*, New York: Bantam, 1974.

Ripple, Paula. *Growing Strong at Broken Places*. Notre Dame, Ind.: Ave Maria Press, 1986.

Robbins, Paula. *Successful Midlife Career Change*. New York: AMACOM, 1978.

Rohrlich, Jay B. *Work and Love: The Crucial Balance*. New York: Crown, 1982.

Russell, Bertrand. *In Praise of Idleness*. New York: Simon & Schuster, 1932.

————. *The Conquest of Happiness*. London: Unwin, 1975.

Ryan, Regina Sara, and John W. Travis. *The Wellness Workbook: A Guide to Attaining High Level Wellness*, Berkeley, Calif.: Ten Speed Press, 1981.

Samples, R. *The Metaphoric Mind*. Reading, Mass: Addison-Wesley, 1977.

Sangiuliano, Iris. *In Her Time*. New York: Morrow Quill, 1980.

Scarf, Maggie. *Unfinished Business*. Briarcliff Manor, N.Y.: Stein & Day, 1972.

Schaef, Anne Wilson. *Women's Reality*. Minneapolis: Winston Press, 1981.

Scholz, Nelle. Judith Prince, and Gordon Miller. *How to Decide: A Guide for Women*. New York: College Entrance Examination Board, 1975.

Schumacher, E. F. *Good Work*. New York: Harper & Row, 1979.

Selye, Hans. *Stress Without Distress*. Philadelphia: J. B. Lippincott, 1974.

Sheehy, Gail. *Passages*. New York: E. P. Dutton, 1976.

————. *Pathfinders*. New York: Morrow, 1981.

Spradley, James, and Robert Veninga. *The Work Stress Connection*. Boston: Little, Brown, 1981.

Thompson, Helen. *Journey Toward Wholeness*. New York: Paulist Press, 1982.

Tsu, Lao. *The Way of Life*. New York: New American Library, 1959.

Weaver, Peter. *You, Inc*. New York: Doubleday, 1973.

Wegmann, Robert. *The Right Place at the Right Time*. Berkeley, Calif.: Ten-Speed Press, 1987.

Woodman, Harry and Steve Buchholz. *Aftershock: Helping People through Corporate Change*. New York: Wiley, 1987.

Woititz, Janet Geringer. *Home Away from Home: The Art of Self Sabotage*. Pompano Beach, Fla.: Health Communications, 1987.